# GOOD STRESS
## LIVING YOUNGER LONGER

# HEALTHFUL
## COMMUNICATIONS

Healthful Communications, Inc.
Juno Beach Professional Building
13700 U.S. Highway One · Suite #202A
Juno Beach, FL 33408
(561) 626-3293
www.healthfulcommunications.com

*Publisher*
Brian M. Connolly

*Associate Publisher*
Eric Zayes

*Managing Editor*
Lynn Komlenic

*Contributing Editors*
Nancy Lyon
Catharine Rambeau

*Typography*
Yanileysi Bailes

*Cover Photography*
Jordi Gomez

*Cover Art and Design*
Jim Scattaregia

coolingtheplanet.org

This publication is printed on Recycled Paper and with soy-based inks. Terry Lyles Corporation replenishes more than the amount of trees required to print this publication, through www.coolingtheplanet.org

Medical Disclaimer: The medical and health information and coaching in this book are based on the training, experience and research of the author and is intended to inform and educate. Because each person and situation is unique, the reader should check with a qualified health professional before following this or any program. The author and publisher specifically disclaim any liability, loss, or risk, personal or otherwise, which is incurred as a consequence, directly or indirectly, of the use and application of the contents of this book.

**www.terrylyles.com**

# GOOD STRESS
## LIVING YOUNGER LONGER
### TERRY LYLES, PH.D.

# Table of Contents

# Acknowledgements

This book was inspired by the influence of many brave individuals whom I have had the privilege to work side by side with around the world and across America caring for those touched by tragedy. When I consider the individuals and groups that have touched me since my last writing, I am humbled by the many names and unnamed faces that I think about daily who make my efforts matter to those that I touch through their influence upon me. Not a day goes by that I don't think about or see in my minds eye those touched by 9/11, the Asian Tsunami, the hurricanes, and our men and women of the Armed Forces that so proudly serve our Country with courage and honor in life and in sacrifice.

Thanks to all those individuals and organizations that support my efforts when tragedy strikes so I can train others how to cope with and eventually overcome difficult life challenges that can touch any of us at any time with or without warning. To those I have encountered in the destruction zones around the world, know that you will never be forgotten by me, because your faces and stories are ever fresh in my mind and in my heart. When I speak or train across the Country I tell of your courage and bravery that inspires me, and those who meet you through my experiences with you.

A special thanks to my sons Brent and Brandon, my executive assistant Migdalia, Sandy, my dad William, my mom Geneva, and sisters Mary and

Becky, Roger, Dale, Chris, Messa Yan, Ginger, and Brian, Eric, Nancy and Lynn who helped publish this work, and are always ready to sacrifice beside me here and abroad when those who are less fortunate are in harms way. Without the efforts of these and others like them, the world would be a very different place, devoid of an illuminated influence I cherish daily and now can share with you who read this book.

# Prologue

The island of Phuket, Thailand is worlds and worlds away from the palm-fringed malls and glitter of West Palm Beach, Florida. Yet when I heard the news on December 26, 2004, I knew I had to go there—by car, jet plane, boat and finally island taxi over the winding dusty Thai roads, all the way to the scene of the devastation. A crack in the ocean floor had opened up, causing a tsunami wave nearly 40 feet high, 180 miles wide and travelling at a speed of 500 miles per hour to crash into three continents. In minutes, the tsunami of 2004 became the largest natural disaster recorded in modern-day history, wiping out hundreds of villages and the lives of 175,000 people from Indonesia, India, and Thailand and Christmas vacationers from several nations.

I walked outside my office and began contemplating the logistics necessary for me to get to the tsunami-torn region to offer my skills in stress recovery training. I've been helping people cope with trauma and disaster relief for over a decade. I have personally witnessed the devastating effects of countless hurricanes in my home state of Florida and elsewhere, and 9/11 in New York City. Many people now know me as America's "Stress Doctor" more than by any other name.

As I paced and paced, stunned by the horrific images I'd seen on TV, my phone began to ring. Friends and colleagues wanted to put a plan in action to help the victims of this tragedy. My New Jersey business associate and friend

Chris Galli, with whom I had done much crisis planning after the 9/11 disaster, and subsequent months training and counseling victims and their families, encouraged me to place my other commitments on hold so I could travel to the far side of the world to offer my services in Stress Recovery.

And so, after a long flight from West Palm Beach to Los Angeles and Bangkok, then on to Phuket, there I was again, landing in the middle of the chaos of yet another disaster zone. You can imagine my shock when a Red Cross worker told me that Thailand was doing fine and was in no need of assistance. I asked a second time to make sure that we weren't just having a language problem and that I'd heard him correctly. Perhaps his words to me were lost in translation. Again, he affirmed that no assistance was needed.

I could only assume by his response that he was in as much shock as the rest of the wave-ravaged coast. Flying halfway around the world only to be told that things were okay after the worst natural disaster in modern history simply confirmed the need for my work. I became even more inspired to apply my unique background experience and skills in stress management to help the Thai people.

For the next three weeks I would be working in temperatures approaching 100 degrees Fahrenheit in the middle of Wat Yan Yao temple, a makeshift mortuary where several thousand bodies awaited identification and transportation to their grieving families around the world. I would be helping the disaster victims and the relief operations personnel dealing with the deadly stress of the event, to help them on the road to healing. In this book I shall be sharing these experiences with you, along with practical techniques and tools for embracing and using stress as a powerful force for your own strength, growth and transformation.

# 1

# What is Good Stress?

I s there any such thing? Can stress actually be good for us? While the phrase "good stress" may sound like an oxymoron, I can assure you that it is not. I have spent my life and professional career studying how stress can and should be regarded not only as something good, rather than negative and harmful, but also as an essential ingredient for healthy living.

Most of what we hear about stress today in the health and other news media, including scholarly and expert literature, focuses on stress as a dangerous and potentially life-threatening force that must be minimized to ensure good health and longevity. But this is only one side of the story – the misleading side. While unprocessed and unprepared-for stress can be deadly, stress that is properly processed is a positive force that can help us move forward and perform with consistent excellence in any endeavor in life.

# Stress Can Be Positive

Good stress can add years to our life span and slow the undesirable and destructive process of aging to help us *live younger longer*. My understanding of stress as a potential force for good comes from many years of working with elite performers in sports, business and the military. They view stress differently than most people. In the sports and business worlds, the stress of competition energizes elite performers and spurs them on to consistent excellence. Military training stresses trainees' minds and bodies. It taps reserves of inner strength and discipline and hones their reflexes, physical abilities and mental processes to such a fine edge that in the chaos of combat they perform with cool precision and unparalleled skill.

Elite performers such as these demonstrate on a daily basis that stress can be a powerful and positive force for good. In reality, stress, competition and chaos are the same thing; they have the same energy expenditures. We view stress and chaos as harmful, but we often regard competition as healthy. This is because most of us don't think of competition as stress. Yet it is.

Stress is stress, regardless of whether the circumstances causing the stress are good or bad. Divorce is stressful; so is the loss of a job or the death of a loved one. Getting married, having a baby and receiving a promotion with a big pay raise also inject stress into a person's life. Unless processed properly, stress can be harmful regardless of the circumstances that produced the stress. The key to health and happiness is not to reduce or eliminate stress, which is neither possible or desirable, but to *process* it. We must learn to use it to our advantage to strengthen us and propel us toward greatness.

If learning to process stress is a key to health and happiness, then the key to learning how to process stress is proper training. Anyone can learn to make stress work for them and become confident and consistent performers—no matter what the stressful situations. As you apply the training presented in this book, you will see how stress can be harnessed to become a powerful positive force that propels us to personal and/or professional breakthroughs that bring lasting changes to our lives and those around us. A fuller understanding of the positive role that stress can play in our lives helps us to navigate life's storms more easily and successfully. We can be healthy, happy and prosperous regardless of how stressful our life circumstances may be.

Have you ever wondered why some people age more gracefully than others? Why some people are still going strong into their 70s, 80s and 90s while many others grow old before their time? It is generally understood that people with a lifelong habit of caring for their bodies and minds through diet and exercise live longer and enjoy life more than those who don't. Another significant factor, and one that is often underestimated, is how well they handle stress on a daily basis.

Our ability to cope with and successfully navigate stress affects our lives in just about every area. It affects our overall physical health, immediately and long-term. It affects our capacity to enjoy life and even has a direct bearing on how long we live. Mental, emotional and relational issues are also affected by how we handle stress.

Proper stress management becomes increasingly important the older we get. Forty-five is the median age at which for the first time deaths by disease surpass deaths by accident. Add to this poor stress management and the risks become higher still. That is why it is so important to learn how to process stress as early in life as possible. Stress is like gravity: we can't escape it, so we must learn to work with it rather than against it.

It is commonly agreed in most medical circles that all of us should have a life expectancy into our eighties based on the current level of medical knowledge, technology and expertise. In reality however, the current average life expectancy for Americans is 74 for men and 79 for women (2003 figures). The difference between the ideal and the reality can be attributed directly and primarily to stress and to our inability to utilize it properly.

# AGING GRACEFULLY...AND SLOWLY

Several factors determine how gracefully and slowly we age. Genetics is certainly a major player. Some people simply have the genes for slow and graceful aging. A life of moderation is another contributory element to health and longevity. I am a total believer in living life to the fullest every day, but living a full life in moderation is a must to living younger longer. By moderation I mean choosing a lifestyle that avoids tobacco, does not abuse food, alcohol or drugs, maintains a healthy weight and includes adequate rest and regular exercise. The ideal time to learn this philosophy of good stress is when we are young, although it is never too late to start.

In helping our children deal with stress, it is helpful to teach them that everything happens for a reason. This will enable them, as it does us, to come to grips with many things that can't be explained or fully understood. It is also important to prepare them for the understanding that life will not always be easy. The sooner they learn this and the sooner they learn to process stress as a powerful *positive* force in their lives, the healthier and happier they will become. For people of any age, stress is a potential stimulus for healthy growth.

Another key factor in the health and longevity equation is the general ongoing stress level in a person's life. Some careers and professions, such as military, law enforcement, firefighting, health care (especially emergency room and trauma unit personnel), teaching, journalism, broadcasting and professional athletics are high-stress by their nature. Many others are less so. Regardless of stress level, it is the *perception* of stress that can either decrease one's lifespan or extend it.

Whatever its source, stress affects every dimension of our lives: mental, emotional, spiritual and physical. For example, stress exhibits certain physical signatures that influence our emotional response to whatever situation caused the stress. Depending on the stimulus, this interaction can very quickly escalate to a dangerous level for someone untrained in proper stress response.

The body responds to a sudden crisis by triggering the release of stress hormones into the bloodstream. These hormones then stimulate a high-negative emotional response such as anxiety. Anxiety feeds the high physical stress level, and the cycle escalates as the person's anxiety is stimulated to higher and higher levels.

Someone trained in proper stress response will know how to recognize the physical and emotional markers, understand the relationship between them and break the cycle and neutralize the anxiety. This is just one example of how understanding how stress affects us can spell the difference between success and failure in stress navigation.

Successful stress navigation is a matter of proper training. Training is what separates the elite from the average in life. Corporate America spends hundreds of millions of dollars annually training people to handle whatever on-the-job situations might occur. Training is the lifeblood of the military, which expends enormous amounts of time, energy, effort and money turning average individuals into elite performers in the midst of high-stress situations.

Understanding the key components of training, which include how we think, how we feel, what we believe and how we respond, makes the difference between those who face challenges head-on with the intention of winning and those who run from life's challenges and crises. This is commonly referred to as the fight or flight chemical response.

# FIGHT OR FLIGHT

The fight/flight response is physical in nature but it also triggers an emotional response that is the product of our programming. Whenever our body perceives threat or danger, it releases stress hormones that deliver glycogen to the muscles and glucose to the blood, thereby increasing oxygen transport throughout our entire body. With this hormonal release, bodily functions that are not needed in a crisis, such as digestion, the sex drive and the immune system, are suppressed so that all energy can be focused on the challenge at hand. This entire emergency "fire alarm" system serves as a built-in survival and self-defense mechanism.

One effect of the activation of the fight/flight response is that the person enters a state of heightened awareness where every sense seems more acute. At first this may be an exhilarating experience – a natural chemical "rush" – but over the long term the condition can be deadly. The fight/flight chemical response is designed to be active only long enough for us to escape the threat that triggered it. The danger comes when the response continues after the threat is past or when it is triggered repeatedly by poor response to daily stress.

Because the chemicals released in the fight/flight response are toxic in large amounts, this self-defense system is designed to be used only at infrequent intervals and for short periods of time. People who are unable to handle stress set themselves up for increasing health problems because stress keeps them almost continually in "crisis mode." The fire alarm is almost always on, flooding their bodies with potentially dangerous levels of fight/flight chemicals. Such a condition can continue for only so long before illness results. People who have received stress-response training or otherwise know how to handle stress well have acquired the ability to turn the fire-alarm switch off more quickly than those who have not been trained.

If blood sugar is unregulated during this process, high blood pressure may contribute to blood clotting problems. High levels of cortisol secreted for long periods of time have been linked with diabetes, heart disease and obesity. Add to this a decreased sex drive and a compromised immune system, and the person's entire mental, emotional, spiritual and physical navigation capacities are strained.

What I have just described is a picture of growing old fast. The key to living younger longer lies in the understanding that stress can be good for us if processed properly. Stress can be a positive energy spurring us on to overcome obstacles, successfully navigate life's storms and become consistent performers of excellence. Living younger longer means knowing how to control our response to stress, rather than letting it control us.

To understand stress and properly utilize it we must first see that it affects us in four primary areas:

Mentally – our thoughts

Emotionally – our feelings

Spiritually – our connection to the 'big picture' and our purpose or goal

Physically – how much energy we have

At any time, we can determine our mind/body alignment by assessing where we are on the target and then making necessary adjustments to restore our balance. Take some time now to assess where you are in your life. Circle the best answers to the questions below:

*1 poor / 5 excellent*

**Mental Zone**

| | | | | | |
|---|---|---|---|---|---|
| How is your ability to focus currently? | 1 | 2 | 3 | 4 | 5 |
| How well are you able to concentrate? | 1 | 2 | 3 | 4 | 5 |
| How well do you handle distractions throughout the day? | 1 | 2 | 3 | 4 | 5 |
| How well are you navigating confusion and indecision? | 1 | 2 | 3 | 4 | 5 |

**Emotional Zone**

| | | | | | |
|---|---|---|---|---|---|
| How well are you managing periods of moodiness? | 1 | 2 | 3 | 4 | 5 |
| How well do you navigate periods of being short-tempered? | 1 | 2 | 3 | 4 | 5 |
| How much do you trust others? | 1 | 2 | 3 | 4 | 5 |
| How well are you dealing with life's stresses overall? | 1 | 2 | 3 | 4 | 5 |

*1 poor / 5 excellent*

### Spiritual Zone

| | |
|---|---|
| What is your level of personal fulfillment? | 1 2 3 4 5 |
| What is your level of professional fulfillment? | 1 2 3 4 5 |
| How satisfied are you with your contributions overall? | 1 2 3 4 5 |
| How connected are you to what's most important to you? | 1 2 3 4 5 |

### Physical Zone

| | |
|---|---|
| Rate your energy quality from morning to evening. | 1 2 3 4 5 |
| Rate your ability to eat every three hours throughout the day. | 1 2 3 4 5 |
| Rate your physical conditioning. | 1 2 3 4 5 |
| Rate the frequency and effectiveness of your daily rest breaks. | 1 2 3 4 5 |

Add all questions together for a total score:

(75 - 80 ) You are operating at peak levels

(65 - 75 ) You are operating at above average levels

(55 - 65) You are operating below healthy levels

(Below 55   Danger Zone ) You could be approaching "burn-out"

It is characteristic of people involved in rescue, relief and recovery efforts to find themselves in the burnout zone after a disaster. Fears come up in the face of unprecedented change and the uncertainty that accompanies such drastic change. And while our mind and bodies are equipped to handle this level of stress for short periods of time, it can be destructive in the long run if it's not navigated correctly.

## TAKING A DAILY INVENTORY

When I work with people, training them on how to consistently thrive in life, I ask them to take a daily inventory. When you awake in the morning take a few minutes to assess where you are mentally, emotionally, spiritually and physically. It is first important to understand *where you are,* so you can make choices about *where you want to go* in order to make the most of your day. As you continue through these pages, I will help you to understand stress as a potential stimulus for your growth. I will teach you how to incorporate the principles of good stress in your own life and make the changes that you want to see.

## ◆ *Good Stress In Action...*

Make a decision *today* to see all stress as Good Stress. See the stress that you encounter in life as an opportunity for growth that will ultimately result in more happiness and success for you.

Focusing on what's important – keeping your eye on the prize – is one of the best tools for navigating stress successfully and easily. Take a moment now to write down your vision for your life, your key values and *why* you want what you want. Reminding yourself of these frequently strengthens you for those inevitable stresses in life.

## 2

# Stress as Gravity

G ravity is a law of physics so basic that most of us hardly ever give it a second thought – until we fall off a ladder or take a tumble down the stairs. Gravity is one of the four basic forces in nature, along with the strong nuclear force, the weak interaction force and electromagnetic force. Gravity is the weakest of the four natural forces yet unlike the others, it has an infinite range. We all know gravity as the attractive force that holds us onto the surface of the earth. Since the earth spins at a velocity of over a thousand miles per hour, without gravity we would all be flung off into space.

Aside from its role in helping to keep us all literally down to earth, gravity serves another important function as well: providing us with necessary stress resistance. Gravity is a perfect example of Good Stress designed in the very fabric of nature itself. Whether you realize it or not, we all depend on the stress resistance that gravity provides for our health and survival. Our muscles become strong and conditioned as they continually resist gravity's tendency to pull our bodies to the ground. Even our heart resists gravity as it pumps blood to all parts of our body against gravity's tendency to pull all of our blood down to our feet. Every moment of our lives is a constant interplay of resistance and balance with the law of gravity.

Gravity as stress resistance is a critical factor to consider in the designing of the mission parameters and training regimen of astronauts. When astronauts travel into space we say that they are "weightless" and in a "zero gravity" environment. Both of these terms, while descriptive, are not entirely accurate. The force of gravity on an object does weaken in proportion to that object's distance from the source of the gravity, but it never goes away. So there is really no such thing as "zero gravity."

Astronauts orbiting the earth are not truly weightless but in a state of perpetual freefall. Gravity is still acting on them and trying to pull them down, but their orbital velocity makes it such that their rate of descent matches the rate at which the surface of the earth curves away below them. They are literally "falling around" the earth.

Prolonged exposure to a "weightless" environment can be devastating to the human body. Over time the lack of gravitational stress resistance that the body needs to remain strong will cause atrophy – mentally, emotionally, spiritually, and physically. This is why astronauts on long-term space missions such as the International Space Station devote a few hours a day to performing specially designed stress-resistance exercises. After their return to earth, they spend months in specific physical therapy and exercise to restore their bone and muscle mass.

# COOPERATING WITH GRAVITY

In childhood we all learn how to cooperate with gravity – usually by trial and error. It only takes one or two jumps (or falls) from a bed or a coffee table to learn that the floor is harder than our head. The bumps and bruises and cuts and scrapes of our childhood teach us that gravity is a force to be reckoned with.

Orville and Wilbur Wright mastered the secret of controlled powered flight by learning to cooperate with gravity. Through many experiments – and numerous crashes – the Wright brothers discovered how to achieve the proper balance between gravity and aerodynamic lift. They transformed flight from a wild dream into a practical reality. Once they understood and began to cooperate with gravity, they succeeded in changing the future of transportation forever.

Just as the Wright brothers crashed some planes trying to defy gravity, many of us today are crashing in our personal, relational and professional lives because we are trying to defy the gravity of a life stress that we have little control over. But like Wilbur and Orville, we can learn to work within the natural laws of that gravitational pull. Putting our faces to the wind, we can use gravity to help us soar to new levels of excellence.

"Falling forward" is the first lesson in learning how to move against gravity. Falling forward is a form of inertia that eases us through doors of opportunities. We are falling forward when we are leaning into success that is not yet seen but only believed in. As we move forward in life our dreams may meet resistance. But understanding the principle of falling forward – moving through obstacles seen and unseen – can convert negative stresses into the life-changing experience of Good Stress.

Elite performers in every field do not look at stress as something to be avoided but as a stimulus continually pressing them to improve. Instead of pulling back from the challenge, they learn to fall forward and embrace it, knowing that the presence of discomfort or pain does not necessarily mean they have reached their limit.

Elite performers learn to extend their limits. Athletes learn that playing through their pain makes them stronger, builds their character and helps them achieve and maintain a sharp competitive edge throughout their performance years. At the same time they discover how to recognize where their true limits are so they can avoid hurting themselves. Training professional and world-class athletes for many years has helped me understand the difference between pain and injury. Pain is a natural stimulus that is a normal by-product of any process of growth and development, whether physical, mental, emotional or spiritual. As such, pain is just as necessary to our growth as good nutrition and sufficient rest.

But it is important to recognize when we have passed beyond pain into injury, which is another situation entirely. Trying to play through injury is dangerous. It can lead to permanent and even disabling damage. Any type of injury is a signal to stop immediately. Get treatment if necessary and allow sufficient time for healing to occur. Many of us go through life playing with injuries, unaware of the serious damage we are causing to ourselves and those around us. We all know the pain of failure, disappointment, disillusionment, betrayal, criticism and broken relationships. We have all at one time or another felt emotionally, mentally or spiritually injured – but learning how to work through this pain will make us better.

Understanding the limits of our mental, emotional, spiritual and physical capacities can actually empower us for growth. The more we learn to play through pain yet stop short of injury, the stronger we will become and the more our capacities will expand beyond their limits.

Cooperating with stress gravity means learning to observe a regular cycle of stress and recovery, stress and recovery. In sports training this stress-recovery oscillation is commonly known as *periodization*. Stress recovery can also be referred to as the work/rest cycle. Whatever we call it, periodization is the key to building our strength for elite performance in any dimension of life.

The daily stresses of family life and parenthood, especially with a special-needs child, helped me learn the importance to my own health of balancing work with rest and stress with recovery. Many of our personal and professional problems stem from an imbalance between stress and recovery. Balancing stress and recovery makes the difference between a good experience with stress and a bad experience with stress.

# ◆ *Good Stress In Action...*

Become aware of the gravitational pulls in your life and see the good in them. Stress will only weigh you down when you can't see it as a wonderful opportunity to soar.

A *gravitational pull* is anything requiring attention and energy that has the potential to create stress. What are your gravitational pulls? Some examples are: children, work, school, finances, social obligations, physical appearance, spouse or volunteer commitments. Make a list of yours now and assign each a number from 1 to 10 (10 is a high level of stress) and then ask yourself these questions:

1. What are the benefits you receive through each of these?

2. How can you reframe the stress associated with these endeavors so that you see them as opportunities for growth, maximizing your positive experience of them?

3. Are there any changes that you wish to make?

Remember that the gravitational pull of our commitments changes regularly. What you could rate as a 10 one month could drop to a five the next month, so visit these questions regularly to orient your mind. This will train you in the process of leaning forward into life each day.

# 3

# Energy Management

Driving southward down the narrow roads toward the tsunami-torn island of Phuket, I realized that all the television images I had seen of this disaster had only scratched the surface of the devastation. Entire villages were gone as if they had never existed. Smashed fishing boats had been hurled a mile inland. Thousands of villagers had no home, no income and little hope for a full recovery.

Many of the Thai people were working tirelessly to rebuild what had once been home but now resembled a war zone. Upon my much-anticipated arrival, my compassion overflowed for the thousands of Thais whose lives would never be the same. A natural disaster that lasted only minutes left effects on the land and the people that will linger for a lifetime.

Over the next three weeks, with the help of a Thai interpreter, I counseled many families and international rescue workers on stress and recovery. My job was to give them the skills to renew their hope and energy toward a recovery process of health, inspiration and a new future for themselves, the people they were assisting and their loved ones.

# INSPIRATION VS. MOTIVATION

What's the secret to living younger longer? It's a matter of learning how to manufacture and maintain vibrant energy that will make the difference between our slipping early into old age or living an adventurous and fulfilled life.

What's the secret of people who seem forever young? The amazing key ingredient in older people who are fully alive and have grabbed life by the tail is that they have learned to build and maintain reserves of good emotional and physical energy that make them look and feel vibrant and alive.

Our modern Western culture is obsessed with living younger longer, spending millions on eye creams to surgical face lifts to body shaping and image contouring. The results are often disappointing because we are focused on the motivation to change, which is driven by external stimuli, rather than inspiration for the process, which comes from within us.

Motivation is *external* stimuli to create *temporary* change, while inspiration is *internal* stimuli to sustain *lasting* change. Have you ever tried to motivate yourself or someone else to no avail? Have you ever tried to "psyche yourself up" to stay on a particular diet or exercise plan or other life-enhancement routine only to relapse after a short time? Such a cycle of effort and failure is not only exhausting and discouraging but is also, in most cases, dangerous to your health.

Have you ever wondered why good motivational speakers are in such demand and why they make big bucks? Partly it is because people have to be motivated over and over again. Inspiration, on the other hand, derives from an inner source that is constantly renewing itself like an artesian spring. The power for lasting change comes from within. A key factor in that process is to understand the concept of Good Stress: that stress can be converted to positive energy, becoming the inspirational stimulus for healthy growth and lasting change. This understanding is critical to our ability to navigate the shoals and rapids of daily life and to grow older without growing old.

Inspiration is as old as life itself. In fact, the Hebrew word *neshamah* means both "inspiration" and "breath." When we inhale oxygen into our bodies, we are literally "inspiring" our bodies to enjoy good health and great potential for a lifetime.

Great performers in every field have learned the difference between inspiration and motivation. They know that inspiration is the energetic force that gets them up early and keeps them up late enjoying life to the fullest. Motivation relates to what we *do;* inspiration has to do with who we *are.* Identifying what inspires you at the very core of your being shows you how to tap your hidden talents and skills, and propel you to heights of excellence and personal fulfillment.

Over the years I have helped thousands discover their "talent inspiration trigger" and then taught them how to "lock and load" and "aim and fire" to consistently hit the bull's-eye of exceptional performance, under pressure and upon demand. Raising a quadriplegic son to the age of 21 has taught me this. Brandon has never spoken or walked in his entire life, and most likely never will. Yet he inspires me to speak and live out my destiny of empowering others with the truths I have learned by administering to his needs.

Brandon is my Life Inspiration. His love of life in spite of enormous challenges inspires me. Getting in touch with my own brokenness through Brandon over the years has taught me that Life Inspiration, which usually stems from some form of personal challenge, is the secret ingredient for igniting inspiration. Inspiration then generates the energy for the passion, motivation, perseverance and force necessary to follow through on any commitment for lasting and healthy change.

# "ENERGIZOLOGY"

Most of us take our energy for granted. What would you do if suddenly one day you woke up without it? I've coined the term *Energizology* to explain the work that I do, which is the study of creating and maintaining energy levels over a period of time. Energizology has been of great interest to me for more than a decade of studying human performance. I generally ponder on a daily basis the importance of physical energy to health, happiness and productivity.

High and low energy levels are symptoms of proper or improper energy management. We all expend and recover physical energy on a continuous basis all day every day. Our bodies generate energy continuously, even while we sleep. The way we utilize that energy on a daily basis can make or break our plans for health, happiness and productivity.

Mastery of our daily physical energy reserves involves learning how to make regular "deposits" throughout the day into our "energy bank." Even though we expend energy throughout the day, we can learn how to replenish that energy by making energy deposits through regular periods of recovery.

Physical energy and emotional acuity are interconnected. Functioning in a heightened state of negative emotions drains our energy and over time will even compromise our health. This is due to the toxic nature of the stress hormones our bodies secrete when we feel threatened or sense danger. Understanding this energy/emotion connection is the key to living a healthy life.

Many people approach each day as if it were a marathon: they get up in the morning and charge through the day without stopping until they drop totally exhausted into bed at night. During the day they constantly make withdrawals from their energy account but they make no deposits. At the end of the day their energy account is seriously depleted. Since even a full night's sleep usually does not fully restore their energy account, they are always operating on an energy deficit. Does this describe you?

A healthier approach is to take each day as a series of short sprints interspersed with brief periods of recovery. In the athletic world this is called "interval training." This approach allows us to replenish our energy reserves throughout the day so that we end the day as fresh and as energetic as when we began. This purposeful and deliberate cycle of physical "oscillation" is the key to our ability to function on all cylinders upon demand all day every day.

The formula for this healthier approach to life is not complicated. It involves learning a few simple energy-deposit strategies that will enable us to recharge and increase all our capacities.

Our bodies have a built-in "energy gauge" that alerts us each morning as to how well we navigated the previous day's stress, and how much energy we have for meeting the challenges and opportunities of the day. When it comes to mastering our physical energy, the issue is not energy itself but rather where it comes from and where it goes. We need to redefine physical energy if we intend to navigate daily life successfully and learn to manage our energy reserves properly.

# ENERGY: THE BODY'S FUEL

How often during a multi-city travel week have I awakened in a strange hotel room physically drained and wondering where I would find the energy to get out of bed and make it through the day. What about you? Do you often feel like staying in bed in the morning because your energy was exhausted the previous day and the last thing you want is to relive that kind of day again? Instead of merely hoping you will have the energy you need for the day, you can be confidant that your body will manufacture it. It will be available to you on demand anytime as needed.

My experience in sports science training has given me great success treating individuals struggling with chronic fatigue syndrome. Here is the first secret: energy control and utilization. The energy to power an automobile comes from a controlled sequence of mini-explosions produced when fuel is put under pressure and ignited in the engine. Without that control, ignition of the fuel would destroy the entire car. This controlled energy expenditure is predictable because the car's system allows the fuel to be released in tiny amounts in a continuous sequence of rapid-fire bursts. The human body also has energy-generating fuel that must be replenished and released in controlled amounts throughout the day for optimal efficiency and performance.

# CHARGE AND RECHARGE

We often regard physical energy as a scarce resource that we must carefully guard and conserve. In reality, physical energy is an abundant resource that our bodies manufacture constantly through food, hydration, and work/rest cycles throughout the day and sufficient sleep. The critical issue is in *how* we expend our energy and in the energy manufacture/expenditure balance that we maintain. That balance determines the level and consistency of our daily performance.

Our physical energy storage and expenditure cycle is similar to the way the battery and alternator function together in an automobile. A car battery has its own self-contained energy supply: a stored electrical charge sufficient for starting the car's engine and operating all its electrical systems. The battery's energy supply is not self-sustaining. Without a linked system to recharge its cells regularly, the battery will drain quickly with use. This is where the alternator comes in.

The alternator serves the important function of recharging the car's battery while the engine is running. Under normal operation the battery remains fully charged and available for the next engine cranking sequence or any other electrical energy demand. If the alternator malfunctions, the battery will quickly lose its charge. The electrical systems will shut down and the car will no longer start. A battery that is drained too far or left discharged too long will lose all its capacity to receive and hold a charge.

Compare this to the human body, which also is equipped with a biochemical and neurological battery/alternator system to keep our energy level fully charged. Why then do so many of us struggle with insufficient energy levels during the day? The problem does not lie with our "battery" – our energy supply – but with our "alternator"-our energy recharging system.

If our alternator keeps our battery fully charged while we are in full operation mode, our body will have all the energy it needs for us to begin and end each day with an energy reserve. Our body is made up of trillions of cells that receive and transmit energy unceasingly throughout our lives. Properly cared for, our body will provide many years of energetic and relatively trouble-free service.

The principles of good stress and proper energy management have very wide applications. They often can extend the length and improve the quality of life even of people with a debilitating physical condition.

# ◆ *Good Stress In Action...*

Look at those areas in your life in which you desire change. Make a list and identify whether each change is externally motivated or internally inspired.

Is there a change that you have been wanting for a while that has not happened? If yes, I can almost guarantee that it is being motivated by an external source rather than inspired from within. Attempting to motivate yourself to do something that is not internally inspired depletes energy and makes you more vulnerable to the stress. Consider instead focusing on your internally inspired changes; they not only generate energy for living, but also for handling stress more successfully.

# 4

# Energy and Emotions

Locating the sacred temple of Wat Yan Yao, which was being used as a makeshift mortuary, took quite a bit of research and several visits to the Thai, British and American embassies on the island of Phuket. The daily journey by car from base camp in Phuket to the temple took one and a half hours each way. Wide paved streets that bustled with local pedestrians gave way to narrower more natural roads where we jolted and jostled our way through the lush maze of tropical foliage en route to Wat Yan Yao. My Thai driver and translator, who I nicknamed "Schumacher," after the great Formula One racecar driver Michael Schumacher, was my only hope for reaching the Temple; we had no map and could only rely on directions from the locals.

We arrived with no trouble and after a thirty-minute exchange between "Schumacher" and the Thai military guarding the temple door, the guards finally opened the gate and allowed us to enter the temple complex. I was immediately assaulted by the overwhelming stench of dead bodies decomposing in the 95-degree heat. The Wat Yan Yao temple served as a temporary morgue: more than 5,000 bodies had lain here for three weeks awaiting identification and relocation.

Getting past the military guards at the gate landed me in front of the New Zealand police force in charge of internal order and DVI (Disaster Victim Identification) supervision. An officer gave me a tour that began with a decontamination drill involving chemical solutions, boots, gloves and heightened hygiene awareness, crucial for maintaining personal health and safety in the mortuary area.

After scrubbing up and passing through chemical solutions to cleanse our boots, I was led past the room where the bodies of victims from Thailand and eleven other nations were laid out on gurneys for identification. International forensic medical teams were on daily rotation to ease the load and to help reduce the chaos and stress around the situation. After several days of laboring with forensic medical teams in the Wat Yan Yao Temple, I was overcome by a chemical substance and was suffering badly from headaches and nausea. It had been sprayed all around the area that separated the Thai corpses from the international ones, and there was no doubt it was toxic. I thought it was odd that I saw no flies, bugs, or any other moving creatures within the temple area so I began inquiring about the nature of the chemical agent. The German forensic team on duty that day told me they'd already shipped samples home to a lab to determine the chemical content.

The absence of life all around the temple didn't seem to bother the international teams assisting with the DVI. They were too busy doing a macabre but necessary job to be concerned about themselves. I did all I could to help them: coached and instructed, talked and listened, and reminded them to drink water and rest when they needed it. I cared for them while they did the work they had selflessly come to do. I will never forget the courage and diligence of these amazing individuals whose work affected thousands of waiting families around the world.

Another gruesome job in the temple was that of the "body slingers" who moved bodies from piles to tables and then, after identification, to caskets. These young eighteen- and nineteen-year-old Thai soldiers had a thankless but necessary job. Yet they passed the time between body transports relieving their stress with laughter and games. They were always smiling, joking and greeting everyone in English as much as possible.

Ninety-five degree heat with little wind and air that was heavy with death was not the best of circumstances, but these young Thais never lost their sense of humor and playfulness. I have thought many times since this experience of how normal these soldiers acted in one of the worst environments imaginable, to their credit. Engaging their sense of humor gave them a healthy way of processing their stress and maintaining their energy levels.

*47*

Stress must be processed or it will cause leakage mentally, emotionally, spiritually, or physically. So when you are feeling stressed out, remember the Thai soldiers' humor and be grateful that you are not working at Wat Yan Yao today.

# *Energy/Emotion States*

Human emotions and the physical energy linked to these emotions are constantly changing. At any given moment we operate from either a high or low energy level with a corresponding emotional state. High energy is linked with an excited, pumped and challenged emotional state while low energy and fear, frustration and exhaustion go together.

A person in a high emotion/energy state has a bounce in his step and high spirits. His face and body language mirror that high energy level. Likewise, someone who is tired will express it in his actions, moping and dragging.

The word *emotion* literally means "to move, to set in motion" or to start movement of any kind. Emotions are the gauges that tell us that we are alive. The issue is not emotions themselves but learning how to understand and navigate emotions. We do this first by identifying the energy level or emotional quadrant we are operating from (high or low, positive or negative) and then using that knowledge to make the transition from how we are feeling to how we want to be feeling.

# THE EMOTIONAL NAVIGRAM

Dealing with emotions can be tricky. The following chart or "navigram" helps us visualize how all our emotions relate to each other. I call this chart a "navigram" because it is an aid in navigating our emotional and energy states.

| **High Negative**<br>*Angry*<br>*Fearful*<br>*Frustrated* | **High Positive**<br>*Excited*<br>*Connected*<br>*Challenged* |
|---|---|
| **Low Negative**<br>*Sad*<br>*Depressed*<br>*Lonely* | **Low Positive**<br>*Calm*<br>*Peaceful*<br>*Relaxed* |

# EMOTIONS

This navigram classifies emotions according to energy levels and locates each in a particular quadrant. The two quadrants on the right house positive energy and emotions, while the two on the left house negative energy emotions. The upper right high positive quadrant contains positive emotions with a high-energy output – excited, connected, challenged and "pumped". Below it is the low positive quadrant of positive emotions with a low energy output – calm, peaceful, relaxed and recharged.

The low negative quadrant contains low energy negative emotions such as sad, depressed, lonely or exhausted. The upper left high negative quadrant contains such high negative energy emotions as anger, fear, frustration and anxiety.

Emotionally, we are constantly moving between quadrants. Sometimes something happens that drags us from one quadrant while at other times we make choices that move us around. Someone may cause us to feel angry, propelling us into the high negative quadrant, but staying there is a choice we make. Circumstances may cause frustration, but how we *choose* to navigate makes all the difference in the world. Choosing between sadness, depression, excitement, calmness and joy is up to us.

My "90/10 rule" says that 90% of reality is perception while 10% is unchangeable. Many people get stuck in a negative emotional quadrant because they don't know how to navigate out of it or because they spend 90% of their time trying to change the 10% of reality that will not change. Gravity is always in force. The sun always rises in the east and sets in the west. We will always have to pay taxes. These are unchanging realities.

A secret to navigating emotions is identifying what is changeable and what is not. We need to identify those things that are within our power to change and learn to let go of those things that are outside our reach. It is not what happens to us in life that defines us but rather how we respond to what happens to us.

It is more of a challenge to be positive than negative – as much as eleven times harder according to some studies. Staying positive emotionally takes work, a deliberate plan and a sustained effort. It takes deliberate intent to migrate from negative emotions to positive ones, and this transition often requires a stress-recovery mechanism. Balancing stress expenditure with stress recovery must be practiced on a daily basis if we are to succeed in living younger longer.

# THE BREATH OF LIFE

There are many ways to recover and move from negative to positive emotional quadrants, but the quickest way of all is through breathing. I realize that this may sound overly simplistic, so I will explain. Oxygen is necessary for our survival. We can live days without food or water, but not even minutes without oxygen; our body cannot function without it. In sports science, fitness is defined by the speed at which oxygen is transferred from the lungs to the heart and muscles and to the blood cells of our body. A person with a high level of fitness can transfer high amounts of oxygen to the body, just like a person with low levels of fitness transfers low levels of oxygen. Can you now see how breathing (the intake of oxygen) is directly tied to our physiology?

The word "emote" comes from the Latin word meaning "to put in motion." Therefore, as breath (oxygen) puts the body in motion, our emotions also put our body in motion.

51

Think about it. When you become scared and need to run from something like a burning fire, your breath rate increases. Why? Because your body needs the oxygen in order to flee the scene so you can return to safety; it was the emotion that caused your breathing pattern to shift. Doesn't it make sense, then, that we can control our emotions and therefore our physiology with particular breathing patterns? It just doesn't seem possible that we could stay angry while taking long, slow breaths in and out through our nose, does it? Take a pause now and take some long deep breaths in and out through your nose. Do you feel the difference? Below are the breath prints for the quadrants; practice these breathing patterns and you will feel the connection:

| Quadrant | Breath Print |
| --- | --- |
| High Positive | *Fast, deep breath in* through the nose and a *fast breath out* through the mouth. |
| Low Positive | *Deep, slow breath in* through the nose, and a *slow breath out* through the mouth. It is a relaxing, calming breath. For the most relaxing breath, make your exhale twice as long as the inhale. |
| Low Negative | *Shallow breath in* and a *slow breath out* through the mouth...the breath of a sigh. |
| High Negative | *Shallow breath in* through the mouth and a *fast breath out* through the mouth...the beginning of hyperventilation. This is the fight or flight breath. |

Whatever quadrant we are in emotionally, we breathe according to the breath print of that quadrant; it is natural, and it is physiological. The fastest way to change emotional quadrants is by breathing according to the breath print of the quadrant where we want to go. For example, if we are in the high negative quadrant – angry or fearful – and want to move to the positive side, the quickest way is to take three high positive breaths: deep in through the nose and fast out through the mouth.

What this does is transport enough oxygen into our blood stream so that our system interprets that we are moving in that direction physiologically. Our emotions must follow because emotions and breath are interconnected. Practice this consciously every day and you will not only gain critical awareness about your body, but also gain control over your emotions. Regulating your emotions is critical to health and peak performance. How does it feel to know that it's this easy to elevate yourself to "thriving" status just like the elite athletic clients of mine? As I said before, it just takes training and practice.

# SETTING YOURSELF UP TO WIN

Now you know one of the quickest ways to work with your emotions and navigate daily storms, through breathing. Below are some additional tips for moving from negative to positive states. Use suggestions on this chart, while adding ones of your own to strengthen those areas of weakness. Practice these with the breathing patterns for maximum benefits!

## *Mental*

- Focus on what is in your control and look for the positive in every situation.
- At the end of the day take a quick mental inventory of the day's victories. They all count no matter how small or large.
- Certain conditions are truly temporary; see them as such.

## *Emotional*

- When you recognize that you aren't handling stress well talk to someone about how you are feeling.
- There is *always* something to appreciate and be grateful for. In an emotionally-charged situation gratitude and appreciations interrupt the negative emotional cycle and put you instantly in a more positive state.

## *Spiritual*

- Focus on your intentions and purpose in the situation – it will give you inspiration.
- Remember the "big picture" while handling the little details of the day.
- Let go of asking "why?" and instead ask "what is the best I can do now?"

## *Physical*

- Take regular breaks every 90 minutes, even if it's just for a few minutes.
- Drink water regularly; it's critical to stay well hydrated and balanced.
- Eat small but frequent meals or snacks of healthy, low-fat, low-sugary foods, with little food prior to bedtime.
- Do your best to go to bed at the same time each night. Prior to falling asleep, focus on positive thoughts and expect a restful and restorative sleep experience.

# ◆ *Good Stress In Action...*

Evaluate your emotional acuity. Think of a situation where you reacted to what happened negatively and lost control of your emotions. See that situation in your mind and ask yourself, how was I breathing? Was it shallow and fast or slow and calm? What outcome to the situation could have been achieved had you taken control of your emotions through breathing? What positive benefits do you see in a practiced and calm response? Next time you find yourself in an upsetting or frustrating situation, practice using your breath to take control of your negative emotions and transition them as quickly as possible to positive ones. You will reap the rewards!

┌─────────┐
│    5    │
└─────────┘

# Stress Recharging

E very day I drove 90 minutes each way to the most devastated area in Thailand, near the city of Khao Lak on the Phang Nga peninsula. My daily drive off the main road into the village areas always shocked my sense of personal comfort. As I surveyed the devastation each day, I could scarcely imagine the screams, horror and chaos of that awful morning.

This area had sustained the most damage because a coral reef near the shoreline pushed the tsunami wave higher than anywhere else in Thailand. A wall of thundering water over forty feet high rushed almost two miles inland, wiping out everything in its path. Local families and tourists were caught off guard and tried to outrun the massive wave. Thousands of families lost their homes and possessions, and some lost family members and friends.

I drove until I saw families gathered together in an effort to make it through another day. My jeep was loaded with food, toys, medicine, first aid and soft drinks, which were a big hit with the kids. The supply containers I handed out always brought smiles of delight and tears of gratitude. As I shared a few moments of a common humanity with these Thai families from Khao Lak, barriers of ethnicity and nationality dropped and we loaded each other's "inspirational triggers."

Each evening I drove back to the base camp in Phuket to restock my supplies for the following day. I did so with mixed emotions and some stressful internal conflict at having to leave those wonderful people for even one night. What an awesome opportunity it was to go in day after day, offering food, care and counseling to those families and relief workers. I was inspired by their courage, good spirit, determination and, most of all, by the renewing of their emotional and physical energy as genuine hope for recovery and a return to normalcy was rekindled in their hearts.

In the midst of the direst of circumstances, just choosing to believe that things will eventually be OK is sometimes all one needs to be self-propelled into a kinder reality. Such is the awesome power of Good Stress. Properly understood and utilized, it can ignite the fire of growth and change necessary for not only surviving, but also thriving again in life. At the same time, understanding the roles of emotions and energy is the key to maximizing the vibrancy and vigor of youth throughout a lifetime.

Knowing how to recharge effectively from stress is fundamental to making the paradigm shift to regarding stress as positive rather than negative. Every day we create and expend energy. Our bodies need frequent deposits of energy in order to navigate through daily stresses, especially in times of extreme duress. If we don't manage our deposits and expenditures of energy well, we'll find ourselves "in the red" energetically speaking. Optimal health and performance require careful attention to the stress/recovery cycle, also known as the work/rest cycle. If we do not do this, we can suffer a physical, mental, emotional or spiritual crash.

# *TAKE TIME TO RECOVER*

Our bodies require brief recovery periods every 90 to 120 minutes throughout the day. This is in addition to the 6-8 hours of high-quality recovery sleep we need every night to replenish our energy reserves. The new understanding of the relationship between stress and recovery is changing the way corporate America looks at employee performance. Most of us work hard every day but rarely think about our need to play just as hard. Play, or recovery, replaces the energy we expend when we work. Do you take time out in the evenings or weekends to enjoy yourself in nature away from home or the office?

A daily recovery strategy does not need to be complicated or time-consuming: We're talking about a 2-5 minute recovery break after every 90-120 minutes of work. This simple practice will put you light years ahead of the majority of people living and working in our modern world. Things like taking a walk around the block, sharing a joke and a laugh with a co-worker, or taking a few moments to stand up and stretch will help to maintain energy levels and concentration throughout the day.

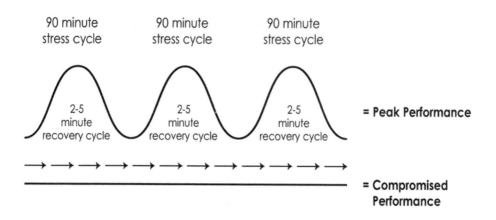

Many of us handle our workday in a linear fashion: We start work at a dead run and bore straight through the day without stopping, sometimes not even for lunch. A graph of that approach would be a straight line, which bears an alarming resemblance to the "flatline" on an EKG or EEG machine. Make no mistake: if your EKG or EEG chart flatlines you are having a very bad day! On the other hand, the graph of a healthy stress/recovery cycle would show an up and down movement like a healthy EKG pattern. This is how we are designed to function every day.

How we are designed to function is one thing; how we are programmed to function is another. Most of us are programmed by our culture and by our employer's expectations to take breaks only when absolutely necessary, instead of when it is absolutely optimal. This results in a drop in productivity and performance quality as the day progresses.

How then do we go about changing our external work habits to allow for stress navigation every day? Each one of us is in charge of our own energy recharging system. And where does our energy recharging capacity come from? Many people believe that the body's energy management is controlled by the mind and emotions. This is not true; our minds and our emotions need regular recharging just as often as our bodies.

Sometimes we talk about the four dimensions of our person – mental, emotional, spiritual and physical – as if they were separate and distinct. But in reality the function of one affects the function of the others. Because these four dimensions are interrelated, we need regular energy recharging to run consistently on all "cylinders." This helps us achieve peak performance while maintaining daily balance, which ultimately leads to more fulfillment and contentment in life.

The energy needed to recharge our system every day is abundantly available through nourishing food, exercise, adequate sleep and recovery time. If we find ourselves consistently running an energy deficit every day, wearing out or running down before the end of the day, the problem has nothing to do with an energy shortage but with how we build up, transport and deliver energy to our system as needed. As humans, our energy transport, storage and delivery system is our daily cycle of eating, sleeping, resting, exercising and recovering.

Developing an "abundance" mentality concerning our ability to recharge our energy each day will transform the way that we think and act during the day. Each of us has abundant resources of energy for working hard, playing hard and enjoying life to the fullest every day. Once we learn how to tap into those energy sources we need no longer worry about "running out" of energy. Instead, we will have not only all the energy we need to meet the regular demands of the day, but also a deep reserve of energy from which we can draw in times when an extra push is required.

I like to compare our daily cycle of stress and recovery to high-speed auto racing. In the Indy 500, Formula One cars race for several hours at speeds over 200 mph. To save on weight and to increase efficiency and safety, these cars have very small fuel tanks. This means they can complete only a few laps at a time before they must make a quick pit stop.

A normal pit stop lasts 7-10 seconds. In this short flash of time, tires are changed, the fuel tank filled, visor cleaned and any other necessary adjustments are made to prepare the car for its next performance cycle. Missing a pit stop immediately degrades the car's performance, sometimes disastrously. The car may run out of fuel or the engine may break down or a tire may fail, with potentially catastrophic results.

Our bodies also have a small energy fuel tank. Its energy capacity can carry us at peak performance for 90-120 minutes before we need a "pit stop" to refuel and recharge. After two hours, our performance begins to drop off drastically. So we need a 2-5 minute pit stop to energize us fully for the next 90 to 120-minute rotation. Believe me, if you implement this simple technique of building regular rest/recovery periods into your day, you will notice the difference in your performance within the first week.

In addition to its immediate health benefits, this approach shows us how well we can perform and how far we can go during a normal rotation, as well as how much "afterburner energy boost" we can apply to meet a crisis situation. In other words, we learn what our limits are and how far we can surpass those limits when necessary. This knowledge can help us avoid pushing ourselves too far, risking injury or damaging our health.

By respecting our stress and recovery cycles and moving between them throughout the day, we build and sustain our physiological and emotional momentum, which leads to peak performance and productivity. This applies to children as well as adults because, from day to day, all of us are performing at something, be it as an executive, co-worker, sibling, parent, lover or friend.

## GET IN TUNE WITH NATURE

Have you ever noticed how much energy children have, running and bouncing with boundless energy every single day? The reason is simple: children are more connected to their natural cycles than we grown-ups are to ours. Consider how often infants need to recharge their batteries. They eat every two to three hours, sleep for several hours, and are awake for several hours. That is their natural daily cycle.

As adults we have lost touch with our internal rhythms. First the demands of school and then the workplace have conditioned us into believing in and adhering to an unnatural cycle. Today we are learning the value for health and peak performance of respecting these natural cycles. We can learn from our children and reconnect with our natural rhythms. If infants need to eat every three hours, then so do we. If they need recovery breaks every couple of hours, then so do we. We may grow from infants into adults but this internal biological rhythm never changes. So to restore a natural rhythm to our lives as adults, it is essential that we reconnect to the innate intelligence we were born with.

As adults, we need less sleep than infants and adolescents because we don't have the same physical developmental needs. But because healing and recovery, whether physical, mental, emotional or spiritual, takes place in recovery cycles, we still require regular recovery cycles as much as infants do. Sleep involves our bodies and rest replenishes our spirits. An adult needs 7-8 hours daily for physical recovery, but the need for regular and frequent rest cycles through out the day still matches an infant's oscillation patterns. Blood sugar and glucose levels are regulated in three-hour modules and must be balanced by regular food intake and recovery breaks. Otherwise our energy levels will diminish.

One thing that prevents us from getting in touch with our natural internal cycles is our strongly acculturated habit of eating three meals a day. Ideally, we should "graze" throughout the day, eating small portions of food every three hours. Meals need to be smaller in size than what most of us are accustomed to. While it is no small challenge to eat smaller portions in our Super-Size-Me culture, it is possible. Smaller meals with an appropriate balance of complex carbohydrates and proteins interspersed with "power snacks" of around 250 calories are just what we need to keep our minds and bodies alert and energized.

Along with nutrition goes exercise. Today most working Americans spend their days behind a desk with little need to move around much in order to do their jobs. Few Americans get enough exercise on a daily basis. With our penchant for eating sugary, starchy and fat-rich foods, it is no surprise that 60% or more of us are overweight and that the levels of diabetes and heart disease have risen dramatically in both adults and children.

One brisk thirty-minute walk every day makes a significant difference in improving our health and energy levels. In addition to the walking, incorporate a fuller, more balanced and varied workout two or three times a week. While a full exercise workout in the office may not be practical or possible, it's easy to get several brief periods of movement during the day. After 90 minutes of sitting behind a computer, our bodies begin signaling to us that we need to move around. If we ignore these signals and fail to move around, our concentration and emotional faculties begin to wane.

Stand up. Stretch. Go get a drink of water. Deliver a memo by hand instead of using the phone or e-mail. Do anything to put some movement into your routine.

Use the stairs instead of the elevator. Park farther away from the building. Walk to lunch. We need to take a lesson from our children and bring our eating and exercise habits into alignment with the internal rhythm of our natural stress-recovery cycle.

# THE SECRET IS BALANCE

Polarities are nature's way of creating alignment and balance. A period of stress should be followed by a period of recovery. Learning to cycle this way on a daily basis can make the difference between success and failure in our lives, careers and relationships. Navigating life successfully is essentially a matter of striking a balance between work and play. Believe it or not, if we want to remain healthy and live younger longer we have to play as hard as we work. I know many individuals who can work as hard as anyone yet don't know how to relax. Even worse, some of them don't even care to know how. They are working themselves into an early grave.

Working hard and playing hard is a time-tested pattern for a great, balanced life. Years ago many people pursued hobbies in their spare time with as much diligence as they pursued their jobs and professions. Some even became widely recognized and respected authorities in their fields of interest with little or no formal education in those fields.

Today we are so busy helping, caring and, pleasing that we rarely find time for ourselves. Whether it's running to ballgames or music lessons, community events or the grocery store, and doing everything else we think we need to do to keep up, it is important to plan time for ourselves. If we don't, our bodies suffer the physical consequences of depleted energy levels and reduced resistance to illness, and our spirits are impoverished. Living younger longer and more happily requires a healthy balance between work and play, between others and self, and between stress and recovery.

## ➧ *Good Stress In Action...*

List 10 healthy things that you can do for rest and recovery that take 10 minutes or less. Some examples: calling a friend, deep breathing, stretching, movement or exercise, visualization, meditation, prayer, reading a book or magazine, writing a card or note, playing with a pet. Monitor your new oscillation cycles in 90 to 120 minute periods and take 2-5 minute breaks to recharge and restore your energy levels. If need be, program your computer with reminders or set a timer. Do this for 30 days in a row and you will be compiling a life-long annuity that pays big benefits.

# 6

# Stress Preparation

A fter a few days with Schumacher, I was familiar with the route to Wat Yan Yao and prepared to make this daily journey on my own. This added stress of driving in unfamiliar conditions on the "wrong" side of a two-lane road with plenty of steep curves actually became a diversion from the demanding days filled with death and destruction. My commute back to the hotel at the end of each day also gave me some valuable debriefing time from my intense experiences at the temple. Although basic and sparsely appointed, my room offered more than enough comfort for me to sift through and process the events of the day. My co-workers, who stayed in different places, had similar opportunities to oscillate between the daily horrors and our privileged nightly respite. With my assistance they developed a great appreciation for these diversions and the critical role they played in preparing them for the following day's work.

Daily stress preparation truly makes the difference between success and failure in any venture. If I failed to take care of myself by getting needed recovery and recharging time, my ability to help others would run thin and potentially threaten their adaptation to some sense of normalcy. Even a short break produced tremendous results.

# *Be Prepared!*

The Boy Scout motto "Be prepared" is an excellent motto for all of us and all of life. Many people simply bounce through life like bumper cars, never knowing when or where they are going to get hit. They spend all their time just trying to make it around the track successfully. When the really big collisions of life arrive, they are caught totally unawares and unprepared, often with disastrous results.

None of us can predict all the storms of life that will come our way. But we can prepare ourselves for life in such a way that those crises will elicit from us a consistent response of excellence and elite performance. We can weather the storm successfully without either losing our cool or squandering our energy reserves. Some people ask whether it is really possible to prepare for stress. "Stress is unpredictable," they say. Yes, but it is also inevitable. Stress is a part of life. If we know stress is coming we can prepare for it in advance even if we do not know the specific form it will take.

Emergency room personnel work in a high-stress environment where they deal with crisis situations all the time. While they never know in advance what emergencies they will face, their education and training has prepared them to deal with whatever comes along, whether it's a heart attack, a gunshot wound, an epileptic seizure or a diabetic coma. The secret is preparation.

Essentially, preparing for stress involves two key components: a commitment to viewing stress positively (as a challenge critical to success) rather than as something negative (as a threat), and an ability to think through and anticipate potential stress before it occurs. One way is to monitor the daily recovery needs that influence energy levels and relationship harmony. The more you can know about your own daily recovery needs, the better prepared you will be to handle stress when it comes. Being prepared for stress is an essential criteria for achieving success. Show me a person's level of commitment to preparation and I will show you that person's capacity to succeed in whatever he or she sets out to do in the midst of stress.

*Prepared people are rarely surprised because they live in expectancy of what is to come, instead of avoiding a future filled with potential exciting challenges.* Preparation takes time and time is money. Success does not occur in a vacuum and it doesn't happen accidentally. Just think of any star performer who worked hard for years to become an "overnight" success. Moses, one of the greatest leaders in the Bible, spent 80 years preparing for his life's work of leading the Israelites out of slavery in Egypt.

Being ready for something great to happen personally, relationally or occupationally involves the ability to believe that something great can happen. Many people who are desperate for something great to happen in their lives are at the same time convinced that it cannot possibly happen to them. Choose to see everything, including stress, more positively and prepare for good things to happen and you will see good things happening. This will create tremendous momentum and you will find it easier to deal with the stresses that do arise.

Stress preparation not only makes us feel more comfortable in readying ourselves for whatever may come our way, but also conditions us to view stress as something good and important to our success. This is the essential paradigm shift that is required for living younger longer. Stress becomes a potential health risk to us when we fail to prepare. Through stress preparation, we can learn to transform daily stress from a dangerous health risk to an opportunity to propel us to the next level of performance.

Elite performers in all walks of life understand the necessity to train at all costs. I've spent years training people for stressful events that may occur by working with them in advance to handle the anticipated stressors. Everyone, from mothers adjusting to broken sleep cycles to teens trying to fit in everyday at school, benefits by training and preparation. New mothers can shift their daytime schedules in advance to allow for more rest. Teens can prepare for peer pressure by working with a trained professional to build a healthy self-image that will produce the confidence to stay true to themselves in spite of the peer pressure surrounding them even into adulthood. Professional athletes, world-class athletes, military personnel as well as others simply working and living their lives need to understand the power of preparation.

If we can practice the same routine or habit consistently for only 30 days, it becomes imbedded in our autonomic nervous system and builds a training mechanism within us that becomes our own "automatic pilot" response mechanism. Military fighter pilots spend thousands of hours preparing to fly missions in war-torn areas to protect our country. Without the commitment and the discipline of "real world simulation training," these elite individuals would not be able to perform their missions with precision and excellence at the desired safety level in times of real crisis. This is the key to staying calm under pressure when every detail matters.

I have watched pilots go through systems checks every single time the same way with the same information and the same criteria before every single flight. To the untrained eye it looks like a lot of redundancy, but to a trained one it is the essence of professionalism and prepared excellence.

Why do pilots take so much time preparing before each flight? Because they operate in an environment with zero tolerance for errors: If anyone makes a mistake, someone may die. That is why, to guarantee success, it is absolutely necessary for every detail to be checked.

I have the privilege of training fighter pilots for the United States Air Force in Stress Preparation and in Post-Deployment Stress Debriefing. I have seen firsthand the time, effort, and energy that goes into their military training to assure a high level of performance. Over the years, I have assisted in enhancing their performance by teaching them about the body's natural biorhythms in dealing with their stress, as well as the critical nature of life-balance in stress preparation.

# LIVING YOUR LIFE'S PURPOSE

A life's purpose is essentially your reason for living and an overriding inspiration for all our actions. Life purpose is not something that you arrive at but something that you live by each day. Everyone has a life purpose. People with a life purpose of helping others learn become counselors, coaches, writers, ministers, professors and schoolteachers; those with a purpose of preserving safety and security become policy officers, firefighters, diplomats or members of the military while those who with a purpose of creating become mothers, business owners, artisans, musicians and marketing executives. Leaders become corporate executives, managers, and government officials, while people whose purpose is to support often find themselves in roles of finance, administration and transportation. Still others have a purpose of guarding the health of others and become doctors, nurses, nutritionists and fitness instructors.

There are many life purposes and often we have more than one. However, there are generally only one or two that really call to you. Some understand their life's purpose from an early age and others have identified it through education, training and experience. Living your life's purpose successfully simply means recognizing its significance in every area of your life and making choices that support it daily.

Under the umbrella of life purpose is your life's work, which is the profession, job or occupation that helps you live your larger purpose. Successful people find the best ways and work to accomplish their life's purpose. They know what they want to do and are determined to do it, preparing themselves mentally, emotionally, spiritually and physically so that nothing will prevent them from carrying it out.

While you cannot prepare for your life's purpose without first identifying what that is, you can become more accomplished at your purpose when you are successful in your life's work. The first and most critical aspect of setting yourself up for success in the area of life work is to do something that you love to do. Automatically, you significantly reduce stress levels by choosing work that is enjoyable. I have always believed that when you do what you love, the money will follow. Once you choose work that you love, being successful at that work is a three-phase process.

The first phase is preparation. The degree of preparation required for one's life work is generally related to the degree to which an error would compromise lives or, on the other end of the scale, enjoyment. The philosophy of "expect the best but plan for the worst" is a key operative for design and planning in such zero-error-tolerance environments as aerospace, medicine, military and engineering that might include everything from the design of submarines to cars to skyscrapers. It also applies to professions with a purpose of maintaining safety and health. In these situations, errors cost lives, so preparation must include an exhaustive look at all worst-case scenarios.

The zero-error-tolerant environment is also at play for a few people in very high-paying or high-profile positions and in industries that are extremely competitive and demand high performance, such as sports and the upper echelons of politics and business. These people, because of their income and position, are under stress to perform at the highest levels and make fewer errors at the risk of professional death (losing their job).

Other work allows for more error and is generally not life and death in nature, but higher levels of preparation will secure a better chance of enjoyment and higher performance. Anticipating potential problems and preparing a contingency plan for dealing with them is smart. But, as with everything in life, there is a point of diminishing returns where the effort and energy you are expending to prepare will outweigh the potential gain of the preparation.

How you manage your life's mission in terms of preparation is up to you. I manage mine to zero tolerance because I am committed to the highest possible performance for my sake and for those around me. When I awake each day, I contemplate the things that are right in my life verses focusing on what may be going less than perfectly. This is the first key to making every day a great day. Even though there may be some bad moments or hours, the key is to have the necessary recovery speed to shift any consuming unhealthy focuses to positive ones for an overall net-positive day. And even though my mission allows for more error than a firefighter, I play it like a firefighter. I aim to be ready in attitude for anything, anticipating potential crises from a calm mind/body state. This is a model of excellence that many have used to become the best they can be in their fields at will and on demand.

Here is a key principle in stress preparation for fulfilling your life's work and ultimate purpose: *No one will ever consistently outperform his or her training.* This means that we must train the way we expect to perform. Do you want to be the best you can be? Then train to be the best! If it you want to be the best skier in the world, you need to train like the best skier in the world. If you want to be the best teacher, train to be the best teacher. Don't train for where you are now; train and prepare for where you want to go, fully believing and seeing your desired reality.

Many people fail under pressure while performing simply because they did not prepare correctly. Over-preparation can give you the confidence to perform well in a pressured situation. The best way to fight off nerves in public speaking, for example, is to be overly prepared, knowing the information and the audience environment thoroughly and then trusting the training instincts to kick in upon delivery by focusing on why you are there instead of how you might impress.

# LIFE WORK IN ACTION

The second phase is the performance itself. This simply means that our performance will reveal how well we have trained. The adequacy or inadequacy of our training will come out under pressure during the performance.

Have you ever seen people who were so cool under pressure that you thought they had ice in their veins and wished that you could be like them? They are the people who have learned to be prepared. Learning from our mistakes is one of the first keys to learning how to duplicate our successes. Quite often, these super-performers have learned their lessons about preparedness through the hard knocks of failure due to *lack* of preparedness.

Performance preparation is just as important as pre-performance preparation. In fact, all three phases of the stress preparation process are equally important. Ignoring any one of them significantly increases one's probability of mediocre performance and even failure.

Remember, none of us, no matter how good we are at what we do, *will ever consistently outperform our training*. This simply means that our performance becomes an indicator of the time and energy and effort we put into the pre-performance training cycle.

Elite performers have learned how to turn performance pressure into an opportunity to excel regardless of who is watching or what is at stake. It may be the bottom of the ninth in the championship game with two outs, two strikes and the winning run on third. Pressure? Just a little! But an elite performer treats that next pitch just like any other. The concentration, calmness and focus come from having thrown thousands of pitches in preseason training, successful executions in other jams, and a delivery ritual that he has typically practiced for years. When that stress comes, he is ready. Some players have reported that their intense focus silenced an otherwise deafening crowd just prior to key play. This is called being "in the zone."

Elite performers live for moments like this, moments that test them because they feel that it is for just such moments that they have been put on the planet. Their purpose, whatever their field, is to be dependable in a pinch, to consistently perform with excellence under pressure on demand no matter what the circumstances. Medical personnel who choose the emergency room versus private practice are a perfect example of people who love the challenge of rising to every occasion; they enjoy the pressure of putting their skills to the test.

I have trained in such a way that I love the pressure of not knowing what's going to happen. That is why I still enjoy live radio and television as a "performance" that offers me the opportunity to trust my pre-camera preparation to speak through me as a calm but accurate responder in pressure. This also prepares me – although with strikingly different stakes and stress levels – for handling crisis in a natural disaster. During high-stress events, information and processes that have been reinforced by good pre-performance training are more easily accessed with mental clarity and emotional confidence and calmness.

The rush that comes from knowing that anything can happen stimulates me to the point of always being on my toes and in a potential zone of excellence.

This love of the challenge that all elite performers share is partly genetic but it is also a learned behavior. Not everybody is "wired" for high pressure/high stakes positions, but anyone who wants to be can be trained for it. To be wired for something means that you have a talent for it. Stress preparation adds a skill-set to that innate talent that will help you in maximizing success and performance. It comes from understanding that we can always expand our capacity for excellence no matter what the situation, as long as we are moving toward the stress opportunity as a challenge instead of a threat. Nothing quite equals the satisfaction of knowing that we have excelled or even exceeded our own expectations.

# DEBRIEF, DEBRIEF, DEBRIEF!

The final phase of the stress preparation process is post-preparation, or post-performance debriefing.

I am a United States Defense Department contractor who regularly debriefs soldiers returning from war, helping them to process mental and emotional pain to re-enter and adjust to a more peaceful environment. I assist these individuals in reconnecting with their families and former lives through a debriefing process of three steps: venting, releasing (or letting go) and realigning (with their healthy and positive vision for themselves and their life). The time it takes to debrief depends on the individual and situation. However, returning to a somewhat normal lifestyle with the help of a trained professional relieves much of the post-traumatic stress of having been in a war zone. One young man returning from the theater of war was struggling with nightmares and flashbacks with little relief. We began with writing stories of what happened and then burning them to release the internal toxic waste for healing to begin. After several sessions of writing and discussing these traumatic events, I helped him to visualize his future in living color and with an excitement to counterbalance the old memories of pain and loss. Articulating a compelling future can radically alter the perception of reality of pain and loss, helping to anticipate a new beginning of hope and wonder.

The debriefing phase is just as important as the pre-performance and performance phases because without proper and healthy debriefing the next conflict, job or relationship will be compromised by a backlash of pent-up energy and unprocessed emotion that can skew a person's perception of reality.

People with a distorted sense of reality cannot experience or live life to the fullest. The best they can do is survive from day to day. This is why it is so important to learn to view stress as something that is good. The three-phase process of stress mastery (preparation, action and debriefing) enables us to move beyond mere survival mode into the fullness of life where we thrive because we have mastered stress.

People always ask me how to find luck. They say, "You've been lucky in your life because of all the things you are able to accomplish." My common response is simple: "It is not luck. It is preparation meeting opportunity." I look at luck as simply an opportunity that has not been met by me yet. That is why I place such importance on training and preparation. Unless we train and prepare, we will miss opportunity when it comes our way. Training and preparation is action that anticipates greatness. When we train and prepare, we are saying that we believe in and are willing to claim the opportunities that come our way as personal gifts of life that validate our desired realities.

Take the example of lotteries in America. More than 80% of all Americans who win more than 1 million lose all of it within two to four years after their jackpot, mostly because they react to the windfall by living and spending like millionaires without preparing themselves to be millionaires. In fact, many of them end up worse off financially. In contrast, when Europeans win the American lotto, they typically do not change the way they have been living. They save most of what they win; they make modest purchases and invest in their futures. In essence, they are better prepared.

Understanding and applying this principle of preparation meeting opportunity is what separates those who perform well under pressure from those who do not. When I debrief civilians or military personnel after some life trauma or crisis, I use a process that involves understanding the three key components to healthy stress processing.

# THREE CRITICAL KEYS TO SUCCESSFUL DEBRIEFING

The first key is learning how to filter, categorize and interpret one's emotions, thought processes and mental images. Remember, emotions can be controlled for periods of time by breathing correctly, moving and exercising on a regular basis, and talking with someone who can relate to your specific needs. Depending on the level of trauma and the severity of the situation, we must defuse those emotions and those visual pictures in order to recover properly and walk through life with a structured balance that keeps us prepared for future performance.

This is a critical part of the stress preparation process because unless we learn how to vent safely and in healthy ways through a therapeutic process, emotional toxins build up inside us until finally they spill over as a form of toxic waste. Have you ever been subjected to someone else's unprocessed negativity, such as political positioning, gossiping, or just plain negative remarks? With emotional awareness it does not take long to learn to recognize the warning signs and avoid the situation altogether.

The second key to successful debriefing is to acknowledge the fact that we have had an experience that must be processed if we wish to release our pain and anguish. Acknowledging the truth of any trauma is a major step toward regaining our health, happiness and productivity. If we skip this phase we end up in denial. Denial will work for only a short time because reality looks us in the eye constantly and rarely forgives us until we can forgive ourselves. When we can forgive ourselves, we can heal from all of our past failures and move into a new and healthy space of living instead of merely surviving.

Acknowledging the fact that failure, trauma or crisis is actually the starting point for any plan of potential success is a major step forward in a successful debriefing process. This stage of the process can take a while to get through, depending on the ability of the individual to let go of any internalized or repressed feelings. Letting go is not easy, as we all well know, but we must learn always to be honest with ourselves. The good news is that we can heal and grow if we acknowledge where we have been and look hopefully and confidently to where we can go as a result of that new learning.

The third key to a successful debriefing is the process itself. This is the ability to continue with the venting phase as long as it takes to come to graduated level of peace with it. Trauma heals over time and the process happens in stages. With the guidance of a professional, you can learn what you need to heal while acknowledging any new layers of the issue so that you heal properly and continue to grow. This final process can go on for a lifetime.

I commonly suggest that people write letters to those who might have caused pain in some way, but to never send the letters. Destroying the letters after the feelings have been expressed is a sign of their willingness to vent and then let go. The important understanding is that life-trauma can actually strengthen and enrich us. These key principles – understanding the power to vent, acknowledge and process – are necessary for any successful debriefing process.

# ✦ *Good Stress In Action...*

Take one issue that you have been wanting to address and write out several points in response to these questions. What do I want? What do I need to do to get it (preparation)? What are the actions I need to take and what are some of the challenges I can anticipate? How do I see myself resolving these challenges?

Remember that you will never consistently outperform your training. So train today like it is your last day on earth and you have one final opportunity to perform. Make it count!

[ **7** ]

# Managing
# Stress

O ne day in the Wat Yan Yao mortuary, I met David, a young and interesting forensics doctor who also worked as a freelance photographer covering human interest stories. David was off to a refugee camp not far to the south and I decided to go with him to see if I could help anyone there.

The refugee camp was a large field with military tents and holding areas for homeless families and individuals. David and I walked past some open tents where children were painting pictures of their experiences during the tsunami. Their paintings, hung up on clotheslines to dry, were colorful expressions of their emotional and mental stress. They were amazing: imaginative depictions of the great wall of water covering houses, boats and trees, and skies filled with birds escaping the watery grave below.

The children were being overseen by a group of Japanese relief workers. I asked one young woman who spoke English to convey to the other workers what a wonderful idea I thought the painting exercise was for the children's healing process. The paintings allowed the children to release the stress and trauma trapped inside, and to vent their toxic memories of the disaster, clearing the way for healing and recovery. Processing internal stress by talking, writing, drawing, painting, music, dance or other forms of artistic expression can transform a wound to a scar.

# STRESS MANIFESTATIONS: IMMUNITY, INFLAMMATION, AND INFECTION

Unprocessed stress of any kind eventually manifests in physical symptoms. These symptoms generally present in one or more of three primary areas: immunity, inflammation and infection – the three "I's."

Prolonged stress without relief and recovery releases toxins into the cells of our body. When the toxicity of our body reaches a certain level of concentration, our immune system becomes compromised and germs break through our physical forcefield of protection. This can result in inflammation that targets previously weakened bodily organs or systems.

Prolonged inflammation can lead to infection in the body that, if not treated properly, can lead to serious and debilitating health problems and even death.

Simply treating the infection with antibiotics is not enough. The symptoms might go away for a while, but unless we first detoxify our body from the harmful stress that caused the original problem, the infection will eventually return, often stronger than before. Eliminating harmful toxic build-up in the body brought on by negative stress is key to avoiding a compromised immune system, thus preventing inflammation and infection that can cripple our health, happiness and productivity.

We live in an over-medicated society. Medical science as a whole has been a great boon to humanity, but our modern society has become too dependent on medicine. We think we can fix every health problem with a pill. A better solution for preventing negative stress and its health problems is to ensure that we get adequate nutrition, exercise, hydration, and rest and recovery cycles on a daily basis.

## *ADEQUATE NUTRITION*

In spite of all the advances in modern medicine and health knowledge, Americans today are more overweight and less healthy than at any other time in our history. How can this be? Because we don't know what or how to eat!

Every week a new study exposes the dangers of eating a certain kind of food. The very next week another study comes out contradicting the first one. Add to this all the experts touting new miracle diets or pills and the result is general confusion regarding healthy eating. And even when we know what and how to eat properly, many of us don't do it because we don't have the time. Life is too fast. Eating on the run is a guaranteed stress builder and a certain recipe for nutritional and physical health problems.

Our society has programmed us to follow eating habits that impede optimal health. How many meals do you think you should you eat every day? Two? Three? Four or more? If you are like most people, you probably answered three, because that is what our society has taught us. But that is wrong.

What if I told you that we should eat five or six times a day? That really is how we should eat for optimal nutritional health. Why? Because eating five or six times a day (or approximately every three hours) coincides with our body's cycle for regulating blood sugar levels. Glycemic levels oscillate in three-hour cycles, so food consumption should be compatible with this. Our long digestive tract is better designed to handle five or six small meals and snacks throughout the day rather than two or three large meals consumed at longer intervals.

Digestion raises the level of blood sugar, the body's fuel and energy source. In response to this rise in the sugar level, the pancreas releases insulin, which aids in the transfer of glucose and amino acids from the bloodstream into muscles and other tissues. As this transfer takes place, the blood sugar level decreases again. The entire process normally takes three hours. Every three hours our bodies are ready to receive another supply of fuel. It is like throwing logs on a fire at regular intervals to keep it burning.

This is why diabetics must be careful to eat something every three hours. Their system is already out of whack because their pancreas does not produce enough insulin to regulate their glucose levels properly. For diabetics, a controlled diet and eating schedule assumes even greater importance. But all of us have a three-hour glycolic oscillation cycle. We all need to eat at three-hour intervals for maximum health, alertness and performance.

If our eating schedule is out of phase with our glycolic cycle, our bodies and our minds will be less efficient. Our mental, emotional, spiritual and physical capacities will be affected. Our minds will wander and we will find it hard to concentrate on the task at hand. Emotionally, we will become apathetic. Spiritually, we will lose sight of our purpose. And physically, we will lack the energy to do the things we need to do.

Common sense tells us that if we increase the frequency of our eating we should then decrease the size of our meals. Eating smaller portions is good advice no matter how often we eat. Most people who eat only two or three meals a day eat more than they should at each meal. Eating large portions three times a day does not compensate for smaller portions six times a day.

Our glycolic cycle does not work that way. Remember, the main purpose for eating is to keep our bodies fueled for maximum efficiency during every three-hour cycle. Consuming more food than we can process during each cycle simply drains our energy and adds to our waistline. Our bodies basically shut down to focus all their energy on digestion. Why do you think you feel sleepy after a big meal?

Peak performers in every field know better than to eat a heavy meal before a game, a performance or a meeting. If they do, their efficiency and performance suffers. It's the same way for all of us: heavy meals limit our performance, no matter what we are doing.

The ideal arrangement would be three small meals a day interspersed with three light snacks. By "small" I mean 700 to 800-calorie meals that balance complex carbohydrates and proteins. A light snack would be around 200-250 calories. Be careful not to fall into the calorie-counting trap. Calories do make a difference but the point here is to change our eating habits to eat smaller quantities more often.

Eating lighter and more often helps us be light and lean and full of energy throughout the day. It keeps our metabolism burning faster, even when we are asleep. Our metabolism naturally slows down as we age but eating smaller portions more frequently will speed it up again. And speeding up our metabolism burns fat.

One key to good nutrition is eating a good breakfast. Many people skip breakfast because they feel they don't have the time or they don't like to eat early in the day. They are cheating themselves out of high energy levels and the opportunity for peak performance. Conclusive studies have shown that children who eat breakfast every day consistently perform better in school than children who do not eat breakfast.

Eating a good breakfast every day is even more important for adults because of our naturally slower metabolism. Because we are literally "breaking fast" after a night with no food, breakfast is the most important meal of the day. So, whatever you do, don't skip breakfast! Get some fuel into your system first thing in the morning.

Another way to improve our general nutrition is to reduce our consumption of fat and simple sugars. The irony is that during the 1990s, health-conscious Americans went on a no-fat and low-fat diet frenzy in an effort to lose weight. During that same decade the per capita obesity rate for Americans actually increased by 15-20%!

What happened? Food companies provided low-fat and no-fat food to meet the public demand, but to restore the taste lost by removing the fat they doubled or even tripled the sugar content of those foods. It was a trade-off that benefited no one except the food companies. Many Americans reduced their fat intake significantly but increased their sugar consumption by as much as 300%! Our bodies store any unused carbohydrates (sugars) as fat. It is no surprise, then, that so many Americans got fatter eating fat-free food. The quickest and surest way to prevent or reverse obesity and improve your general health is to reduce your consumption of fats and simple sugars.

# ACCELERATOR AND BRAKE

Smart and healthy nutrition boils down to striking the proper balance between good sources of proteins, carbohydrates and good fats, the three basic categories of nutrients. Nutrients from these foods link up with specific chemicals in our blood, which then are carried to the brain to perform their specific tasks. Proteins speed up our brain and carbohydrates slow it down, as do accelerator and brake pedals in an automobile. Since our brain chemistry affects every dimension of our being, it is critically important that our diet consists of the best ratio of protein, carbohydrate and fat intake in such a way as to ensure optimal brain function.

Protein, the "accelerator," gives us alertness by speeding up brain transmission. During digestion, chains of amino acids that comprise proteins are extracted from our food and passed into the bloodstream. Tyrosine, a specific amino acid in the blood, extracts the chemicals dopamine and norepinephrine, stimulants that bring alertness to the brain. Alertness is important for proper brain function, but too much alertness is unhealthy. Dopamine and norepinephrine in excess amounts can cause distractibility, hyperactivity, anxiety and sometimes paranoia. People with Attention Deficit Disorder (ADD) or Attention Deficit Hyperactivity Disorder (ADHD) generally overproduce these chemicals.

How do people with abnormally high levels of these chemicals bring them under control? There are only two ways: by reducing protein consumption (increasing consumption of complex carbohydrates) or by exercising to burn off the excess protein. Reducing protein consumption means moderating one's intake of high protein foods such as meat, fish, nuts, cheese and eggs.

Complex carbohydrates decelerate the brain; they are the brain's "brake pedal." It's important to distinguish between complex ("good") carbohydrates and simple ("bad") carbohydrates. Complex carbohydrates consist of fruits and vegetables, whole grain and multi-grain breads such as wheat, rye and pumpernickel, "dark" rice such as wild or long-grain brown rice, and alternative pastas such as buckwheat noodles and bulgar wheat.

Simple carbohydrates include all sugars, potato chips, ice cream, candy, pastry, cookies, pies, cakes, fried foods, as well as "white" bread, rice or pasta. These are less nutritious because they convert rapidly to sugar in the blood, significantly increasing the glycemic index. In any healthy diet, simple carbohydrates should be consumed infrequently, as they offer little to no nutritional value and lead to cravings and excessive food consumption.

Complex carbohydrates, on the other hand, are the kind we need in abundance and continually for body fuel, good nutrition and to balance out the protein "accelerator." When complex carbohydrates pass into our bloodstream, an amino acid called triptophan converts them to serotonin, a brain chemical that helps us feel relaxed, calm and peaceful. One cause of depression is insufficient levels of serotonin. Antidepressant drugs, or serotonin reuptake inhibitors, increase serotonin levels in the brain. Essentially, complex carbohydrates are natural antidepressants.

The diet of the average American is too high in simple carbohydrates and too low in complex carbohydrates. This is probably the single greatest factor in the obesity epidemic in our country today. Our body craves complex carbohydrates; it is how our system is designed. If we try to satisfy that craving with simple carbohydrates, all we succeed in doing is tricking our body into feeling satisfied without giving it the nourishment it needs.

Consider chocolate, for example. Many people, especially women, insist that they have a chocolate craving or even a chocolate addiction. While this may seem very real to them, it is a deception. Chocolate seems to satisfy because, as a simple carbohydrate, it metabolizes rapidly and gives a quick "high." Chocolate, therefore, easily becomes a comfort food.

I often advise clients that if they feel they must eat chocolate, then eat dark chocolate, and in moderation. Dark chocolate contains flavonoids that help strengthen the immune system. Satisfy the body's need with a complex carbohydrate, such as a piece of fruit, and then, as a treat, enjoy a little bit of chocolate.

In all things nutritional, as with chocolate, moderation is the key! A proper ratio of complex carbohydrates, protein and fat is essential. Consult a nutritionist or dietician to determine the best program for you. For best results, eat protein in the early part of the day; proteins help us be alert and run on all cylinders. At the same time we should balance our protein intake with complex carbohydrates throughout the day, to keep those alertness chemicals from shifting our system into "afterburner" mode until we "flame out."

Scott Sharp's pit, Nashville Super Speedway, 2005

Scott Sharp & Dr. Terry Lyles, Homestead, Florida, May 2005

Child's painting of
Asian Tsunami

Boy painting in a refugee camp after Asian Tsunami,
Pang Nag, Thailand

Memorial for Asian Tsunami victims, Phuket, Thailand

Children's tsunami paintings hanging out to dry, Pang Nag Thailand

Dr. Terry Lyles at a fishing village, Pang Nag, Thailand

Child's drawing of Asian Tsunami

Dr. Terry Lyles on
location in Pang Nag,
Thailand

Boat washed ashore by Asian Tsunami,
Pang Nag, Thailand

Wreckage from Asian Tsunami,
Pang Nag, Thailand

A "hole" where bodies are being discovered, Pang Nag, Thailand

For this same reason we should avoid eating protein just before bedtime. Even if we fall right to sleep, the protein will keep our brain active, preventing us from resting as completely as we should. Eating complex carbohydrates, on the other hand, will slow our brain down, calm us and help us prepare for a good night's sleep. Even then we should not eat immediately before going to bed, but allow 60-90 minutes for digestion.

# DIETING WITH THE EYES

Isn't it ironic that over the past few decades Americans have been on a diet craze and yet we have grown fatter as a people? Some diets fail because they are bogus; they simply do not work. Others fail because they are unsustainable. Either they are too restrictive regarding what the dieter can and cannot eat or they are too complicated to follow. Busy people are not going to count calories or measure food portions.

More importantly, diets don't work because they are approached as only a short-term solution. Most people begin a diet with an end date in mind – a date by which they expect to lose a determined amount of inches or weight. So the perspective from the beginning the diet is: Eating this way is painful but it's not forever! No wonder that diets fail. Eating well and the health that goes along with it is a lifelong endeavor. Finding the inspiration for eating well comes down to caring enough for ourselves and our bodies to make the necessary lifestyle adjustments that are both healthy and sustainable.

# EATING FOR LIFE

Complex carbohydrates calm us down but they are also important because they give us energy. Our physical energy levels come from complex carbohydrates. This is why we never see spectators at marathon races offering runners barbecued ribs or fried chicken. Instead they hand out water, vegetables, fruit, fruit juice or some other source of complex carbohydrates to provide the runners with the energy they need to finish the race.

High-protein, low-carb (complex or simple carb) diets are unhealthy and ineffective for long-term weight stabilization. They can also lead to rapid energy loss. The excess protein and fat can only be burned off with high amounts of exercise. Moreover, these diets often lead to other types of health and nutritional problems.

There is an easier more common sense way to balance the proteins and complex carbohydrates that we need in the correct proportions. It does not involve measuring portions or counting calories. Better yet, there are no foods that are totally off-limits. Again, moderation is the key, along with intention: eating with an eye to fueling our body only for what it will need for the next three hours until the next fueling pit stop. The success of this approach depends also upon the frequency and size of our meals. This method is so effective that I use it myself and prescribe it for my performance clients. In a way, you could call it dieting with the eyes. I usually refer to it simply as the "eyeball method."

Success with the eyeball method involves three basic understandings. First, understanding the difference between proteins and simple and complex carbohydrates and which foods fall into which categories. Second, understanding how each food will affect our system – whether it will act as an accelerator or as a brake during the three-hour cycle. Third, understanding how each food will affect our performance during that same period. With this knowledge we will be able to make informed and intentional decisions regarding what we eat and when.

In principle, the eyeball method is simple. The biggest challenge in making this approach work is learning to think differently about food. Most of us select the food we eat based primarily on taste. With the eyeball method, we choose foods and combinations of foods based on their function in the body, either as an accelerator or a brake. It is a matter of thinking ahead and always keeping in mind the necessary balance between proteins and carbohydrates.

Imagine that you are standing in a buffet line. The first thing to do is to locate the protein foods and the carbohydrate foods to see what choices are available in each category. Next, separate the simple carbohydrates from the complex carbohydrates. Finally, make your food selections carefully to ensure the proper ratio between proteins and carbohydrates.

The optimum ratio will vary from person to person because we all have different metabolisms. Finding the right mix for you may take some time and experimentation. Tune into your body; it will tell you when something works for you or not. If you find that you can barely keep your eyes open after a meal then take notice and make adjustments.

Following the eyeball method, you may go through the buffet line and choose a chicken breast or some lean roast beef for your protein source. For balance on the carbohydrate side, you might choose a couple of vegetables, such as green beans and carrots. If you want some bread, check first to see whether it is white bread or whole or multi-grain bread. If it is white bread, you may choose to pass on it, particularly if you plan to eat dessert, which will most likely be a simple carbohydrate also. If your vegetables and "dark" bread makes your plate a little heavy on the carbohydrate side, you may choose an additional protein source, such as a little bit of cheese, to bring everything into balance.

Once you become comfortable with this approach it will quickly become second nature. One significant benefit to the eyeball method is that it places no foods off-limits. Enjoy all the foods you like, but focus on moderation and balance. And remember to keep the portions small: You will be eating again in three hours.

## *Adequate Exercise*

Exercise goes hand in hand with proper nutrition in controlling obesity, improving overall health and enabling us to convert bad stress into good stress. Diet alone is not enough. It is the combination of diet and regular physical activity that makes the real difference for our long-term good health and our ability to process stress successfully.

Getting the proper amount of exercise need not be expensive or time consuming, if we learn to incorporate physical activity into our daily routine as much as possible. Four simple things practiced consistently and regularly are all it takes to ensure that we have enough physical activity to help us stay healthy.

The first of these is cardiopulmonary, or aerobic exercise, which stretches and conditions the heart and lungs. A healthy cardiopulmonary system increases our capacity to handle stress. Since stress is a fact of life, we need to train ourselves to deal with it.

Aerobic exercise doesn't have to involve hours and hours in the gym or pounding pavement. Three or four 25- to 40-minute sessions a week are sufficient. That is less than three hours a week that can help add years to our lifespan as well as enhance the quality of our life. Cardiopulmonary exercise is any physical activity that elevates the heart and respiratory rates: walking, jogging, bicycling, swimming, etc.

The most effective method of cardiopulmonary training is oscillatory or interval training. Linear training involves exercising at a high intensity for a sustained period. Interval training begins with a slow warm-up followed by a cycle of fast-slow, fast-slow, or stress-recovery, stress-recovery. Interval training is easier and more fun than linear training, and it achieves results more quickly.

In addition to deliberate exercise, we can incorporate healthy physical activity into our daily routine in ways that don't even seem like exercise. When shopping or running errands, avoid parking close to the entrance; walking is excellent exercise. Whenever possible, take stairs instead of elevators or escalators. At work, stand up every couple of hours and take a stretch break or go for a short walk – anything to inject extra movement into the day's routine. Every little bit helps. Some activity is better than none and often the best way to make a large change in our life is to begin with small steps.

My 80-year-old father never "exercised" a day in his life, but he was in excellent condition for someone his age. For 30 years he worked a job that had him on his feet moving all day long. Even though he is no longer with us, he enjoyed the benefits of a lifetime spent being physically active.

Another important aspect of an exercise program is regular stretching. Many people who begin an exercise regimen quit after a short time because the pain becomes too intense. One common reason for this pain is their failure to begin their workout with stretching exercises to develop flexibility. Unconditioned muscles and tendons will indeed rebel if forced into sudden vigorous activity. Stretching helps prepare them more gradually for higher intensity demands. Stretching is light cardiopulmonary activity that generates sweat if done vigorously. Yoga-type stretching of our legs, arms and backs and rotating our midsection are all positive activities conducive to building physical flexibility. They stimulate our muscles and help prevent stiffness, thereby reducing the risk of injury during workouts.

Lower back pain causes many people to drop out of an exercise program. Strengthening and conditioning the abdominal muscles, which help support the lower back, can alleviate this pain. The most effective way of conditioning these muscles is through a daily routine of abdominal crunches. Our abdominals act as "shock absorbers" when we walk or run, and the stronger they are, the better they work. If they are weak they cannot absorb the shock of repeated impacts with the ground, and this stress is passed to other parts of the body, such as the lower back. For this reason it is important to take up regular abdominal conditioning at the same time we begin cardiopulmonary exercise. While other muscle groups require 24-36 hours to recover after a workout, our abdominals recover in only 12 hours, which means we can exercise them every day.

The abdominal crunch strengthens the stomach by "crunching" together the associated muscles in the abdomen. To perform this exercise, lie flat on your back with your legs bent and your feet flat on the floor. This takes the pressure off of your lower back. Place your hands behind your head and bend slightly at the waist in a series of controlled curls, crunching the abdominal muscles together. These are small movements. Your shoulder blades should not even leave the floor. Don't pull yourself up; let your abdominals do the work. Start slow and easy with 20 to 30 a day with the goal of working up to 100 a day. You should notice a difference almost immediately.

In addition to cardiopulmonary training, stretching and abdominal crunches, I also recommend a regular regimen of resistance training, preferably 3-4 times a week, 30-40 minutes a session. This might include push-ups, curls, weightlifting, Nautilus machine, etc. Your personal program can be as simple or as elaborate as your inclination and budget dictate. Work out at home or at the gym. Use professional bodybuilding equipment or just work with the weight resistance of your own body. The choice is yours. A simple inexpensive elastic "dyna-band" or exercise band brings excellent results. Versatile and easy to store and carry, it can work your biceps, triceps, chest, back and even your legs.

Whatever workout regimen you choose, be consistent. Consistency is the key to success. You'll be amazed at how quickly you will feel better physically, have more energy and mental sharpness. And at how much better equipped you will be for quickly converting bad stress into good stress.

# *ADEQUATE REST AND HYDRATION*

America is a land of plenty, yet two chronic deficiencies afflict many Americans regardless of region, race, gender or socio-economic status: inadequate rest and inadequate hydration. Most of us do not get enough sleep or drink enough water. Sleep deprivation is an ongoing problem for millions of us. It adversely affects our physical stamina, mental acuity, emotional equilibrium and spiritual sensitivity. We may become so accustomed to our sleep pattern and schedule that we don't even recognize sleep deprivation as one of the causes of our problems. Because it weakens us in every dimension, sleep deprivation also hinders our ability to process stress successfully. When we are deprived of sleep we will likely turn to caffeine or sugary foods to satisfy our need for energy, when what we really need is rest.

Compounding our sleep deprivation is our failure to take frequent rest and recovery breaks throughout the day. The truth is that we simply cannot function at peak performance and efficiency without allowing times throughout the day for recharging our batteries. We cannot achieve peak performance without adequate rest and recovery.

Remember, your body operates on 90-minute oscillatory cycles. Every 90-120 minutes you need a little bit of R and R. Take a walk. Grab a power nap. Get a drink of water. Listen to music. Eat, if you are hungry. Two to five minutes is sufficient for most breaks – just enough to get a change of pace and reset your mental faculties for the next cycle. Longer breaks may be needed depending on the demands of the activities on hand.

Including time for regular recovery breaks during the day is easy once you are committed to it. Solving chronic sleep deprivation is more complicated and requires much greater determination and effort. Part of the secret is learning to work with your built-in internal body clock, not against it. Sleep deprivation can occur when our sleep cycle and habits run counter to our body's natural rhythm. The result is chronic fatigue, reduced stamina, impaired mental acuity and even a compromised immune system, leaving us more vulnerable to illness.

Because of the natural rhythms of our body, it responds well to routines, particularly sleep routines. Here are a few simple steps to help improve your sleep and eliminate sleep deprivation.

Establish set times for going to sleep every night and getting up every morning and follow them as consistently as possible. Your body will adjust rapidly to this routine and you will sleep better and get more restful sleep.

Avoid mental and emotional stimuli immediately before bedtime. Allow your mind about half an hour to slow down and relax. Don't subject yourself to anything that will shift your mind into analytical mode. Instead of watching TV, read or listen to calming music.

Limit your bedtime reading to light, entertaining or personally fulfilling material: a novel or short story, a hobby magazine, spiritually inspiring literature etc. Bedtime reading should relax your mind.

Avoid eating 90 minutes before bedtime. Unsettled digestion can keep you awake.

Keep your bedroom as cool as possible yet still comfortable. It's easier to fall asleep in a cool room than in a warm room. If you get cold, you can always throw on an extra blanket. Another bonus to sleeping in a cool room is that the body will generate heat to warm up, which burns fat.

Sleep with all the lights off or only a small nightlight. Too much light will keep your senses too alert for a deep sleep.

If you wake up during the night, resist the temptation to look at the clock. Reading the time will only send your mind into analytical mode, making it difficult for you to go back to sleep.

When the morning alarm wakes you, avoid hitting the snooze button. Get up at your scheduled time and turn the lights on immediately. Become active as soon as possible. All these things will help you wake up more quickly.

Inadequate rest is one common deficiency among Americans; inadequate hydration is another. Our nation is hooked on sugary sodas, as well as coffee and diet sodas with caffeine that severely dehydrate the body. Dehydration affects our ability to perform in every area. In addition to balanced nutrition, we need to drink plenty of water throughout the day—anywhere from 32 to 48 ounces depending on your size. It's okay to drink other things as well, but if you do drink caffeinated beverages you must be sure to consume even more water to counteract their negative effects.

Stress is an inevitable part of life. A healthy, well-conditioned and rested body will be a great ally in helping you convert bad stress into good stress!

# ◆ *Good Stress In Action...*

Commit to making one permanent shift in the area of food, exercise or sleep. Determine what it is you want to do and the actions required. Prepare for this change by anticipating challenges and putting a system in place for success. Remember that something becomes a habit in a very short time when we are inspired and prepared. Just see it for yourself and fall forward into the success that you envision, while creating and maintaining higher and higher levels of physical energy.

# 6

# Work Stress

D riving through Thai villages looking for families and individuals to assist with supplies or treatment, I saw an area that the tsunami had turned into a huge muddy lake. Scattered around its edges were small groups of people. They watched as Thai solders dug through the mud that covered the remains of destroyed houses, looking for bodies and remains that might connect them with missing friends or family members.

Off in the distance was one of the oddest sights I saw in Thailand: a 70-foot fishing boat resting against a house roughly a mile and a half inland. I thought of Noah's Ark on Ararat after the Flood. Once again, I was awestruck by the tremendous force of a 40-foot wall of water crashing onto the beach with no warning and no mercy.

Every day was filled with mental, emotional, and physical stress related to the relief work I was participating in. And while the chances are pretty slim that we'll ever encounter the kind of stresses facing the relief workers at Wat Yan Yao temple, no matter what kind of work we do, work stress is something we all deal with every day. Work stress has the same physiological, neurological and psychological effects on our bodies as stress from any other source and must be processed properly if we want to avoid health problems and interpersonal relationship difficulties.

Many problems in job performance can be traced directly back to unresolved workplace stress issues. This is a universal problem among working people everywhere. No matter where I go, people who learn that I am a Stress Doctor ask, "When can I sign up?" In recent years stress in the workplace has increased, and the phrase "a job to die for" has in many cases become literally true.

It doesn't have to be that way. Workplace stress can be processed and navigated successfully through training. It means developing a different concept of stress that enables us use adversity to strengthen rather than to weaken us. My corporate clients range from Fortune 100 companies to small business owners with only a few people on staff. Whether it is a school system dealing with young children and the stresses they encounter in the hallways and classrooms, or the faculty and administrative staff and the pressures of parent meetings, or the executives I coach on a monthly basis, stress must be handled strategically in order to achieve consistent excellence.

*"My job would be great if it weren't for the people."*

One of the most common problems in the workplace is stressful interpersonal relations. We might as well accept the fact that there will always be people who are never going to act as we would like them to. There will always be that loud character in the next cubicle who is forever telling off-color jokes, or the insecure supervisor who always takes credit for other people's ideas and work. Since we cannot escape these people, we need to learn how to navigate this stress through relationship awareness. Let's be honest: Nobody likes stress in the workplace, but it certainly makes life at work interesting! That can be an asset, particularly when we understand the principles and concepts of Good Stress.

People issues are a constant reality in corporate America because as long as people work together in the same setting there are bound to be conflicts. We all come to work with our own different agendas and ideas of how things ought to be. We will rarely all be in agreement on everything, so we must learn to live with the differences. Our problem is *not* the people we work with. Our problem is learning to navigate through the stress that workplace conflict causes. Learning to navigate *with* colleagues is key to our success in the workplace.

I often tell people that normal is what we see in the mirror; outside of that, we are all on different levels of strange. Part of successfully navigating people issues in the workplace is learning to celebrate our differences and appreciate the unique perspectives, and therefore the unique contributions, we each can bring to the work environment and the project at hand.

*"What we have here is a failure to communicate."*

One of the memorable lines from the Paul Newman movie *Cool Hand Luke* is when the warden of the prison work farm, after multiple attempts to rein in a troublesome inmate, says, "What we have here is a failure to communicate." In other words, "I'm not getting through to you. It's time to use sterner measures."

Failure to communicate is one of the primary causes of people issues in the workplace. Navigating these issues successfully involves understanding the people we work with. In order to understand them we must be able to communicate effectively and clearly. Effective communication is like a good game of tennis: I serve the ball and you return to me, and then I return it to you. Each person who is communicating is motivated to maintain this interaction without trying to make the other person miss the return. In other words, each communicator is motivated to keep the ball moving.

There are three basic rules for effective communication. The first is that we must *connect* with people before we can ever expect to influence them in some way. No matter how good or important our idea or message may be, if we don't connect with our intended audience communication will not take place.

Connecting involves things like making direct eye contact and matching body language, tone of voice and energy levels. Essentially, connecting means being able to relate to others and allowing them to relate to us in the same way. Most of our people issues would disappear if we communicated clearly, and communication begins with connecting.

The second rule of communication is *influence* that can transmit our message in such a way that others will understand our viewpoint even if they disagree with it. This means speaking or writing clearly and with passion and conviction in as simple terms as possible, to minimize the likelihood of misunderstandings. Don't use a 10-dollar word when a 25-cent word will do. Find a common frame of reference with the audience through which to communicate the message.

The third rule of effective communication is leading someone on a journey through a new idea or viewpoint and creating a channel for feedback. We need a way of determining that what we said was understood the way we meant it. Leading someone on a journey requires connecting to build trust, then influencing him or her through a passionate and energetic discourse that challenges the listener instead of threatening him. Allowing for feedback is critical for good communication. If we have communicated well, anyone should be able to repeat what we said. Otherwise, no communication has taken place.

The same thing is true in listening, which is another vital component of communication. When we listen to someone else, instead of thinking ahead to what we are going to say next we should pay careful attention to their words. We should be able to respond by saying something like, "Here is what I heard you say" and then repeat what they said. The more we learn and practice good communication skills, the more confidence others will have in us and the more influence we will have over them.

# CONFLICT RESOLUTION

No discussion of people issues in the workplace is complete without addressing the subject of conflict resolution. Whenever two or more people work together, eventually conflict of some kind will arise. Conflict resolution is more than simply choosing one side or position over another. True conflict resolution means finding a way of connecting opposing viewpoints somewhere in the middle to arrive at a compromise that everyone can live with. I am often called in by companies to do conflict resolution between individuals and work teams.

One common source of conflict is what, in the communication business, is called "transference." Transference is the negative energy and emotions that often flow between two individuals or groups engaged in an unsuccessful communication effort. It generally occurs when one side tries to force the other to see its point of view.

Transference takes place when one side skips the connection phase of communication and tries to establish its position through force. If this tactic works and the other party yields, the negative buying-in process is called counter-transference. The end result is an outwardly harmonious but inwardly dysfunctional individual or group that is disgruntled over having to yield its position unwillingly. Such a situation does not bode well either for future communication or healthy interpersonal relations. Its negative effect on productivity and performance should be obvious.

In some ways transference is like forced conversions, as when minorities are forced on threat of death to "convert" to the majority thinking and beliefs. The coerced people may comply, but their conversion will remain superficial. As Samuel Butler said, "He that complies against his will is of his own opinion still."

Because of the powerful negative emotions surrounding it, transference can be an extremely tricky thing to understand and interpret. One of the goals of conflict resolution training is to help people recognize the characteristics of transference so they can identify it when it occurs and shut it down. If transference is eliminated, there will be no counter-transference. Preventing this negative action/reaction process makes an enormous difference in promoting healthy communication and the positive interpersonal relations that go along with it.

While transference is a significant source of tension on the job, most workplace conflict stems from the lack of a stress recovery system built into the workday. A stress recovery system allows individuals and work teams to recharge their batteries while at the same time diffusing potential negative situations. I've already mentioned the importance of regular stress recovery, but it bears repeating here in relation to the workplace.

Stress recovery and the establishment of recovery zones in the workplace promote better health among employees and can help eliminate most stress-related conflict. Every employee, manager and executive needs recovery time every 90 to 120 minutes, two to five minutes throughout the day, to process stress successfully. Every workplace environment needs a recovery zone: a place where workers can find healthy snacks, plenty of water and a soothing environment in which to relax, recharge and decompress from job stress, interpersonal conflict or other issues. This recovery zone is a major step above the traditional break room. I have helped many companies create recovery zones to assist them in managing people issues. Again, all workers need a chance to escape occasionally for a few minutes into a peaceful oasis where they can recharge their batteries free from stressful surroundings or intimidating situations.

# "I," "We" and "It"

In the course of my consulting work I have discovered that the number one reason why people leave their jobs in America is because of problems with the person they report to. Stress with the boss is frustrating and can become overwhelming if it occurs on a regular basis. Stress with the boss often occurs because the boss has no training in dealing with stress and this affects the workers. My usual protocol in stress utilization training for businesses is to begin at the top with the executives and upper-level management, and work my way down through the mid-level managers, team leaders and individual workers. This ensures that when it comes to stress relief and recovery, everybody in the organization operates by the same rules.

Working with Fortune 500 management teams on stressful topics such as healthy and effective communication techniques is always interesting. Years ago, I worked with a senior executive who had been challenged with the task of heading up a new venture for the company. He had a new team reporting to him that would test his leadership and communication skills along with those of the entire team. I commonly teach that communication is the lubrication to healthy and functional relationships at work and at home; without it, anything that can go wrong usually does. The executive had to step out of his comfort zone and co-create a vision with the team that would be both inspiring and in alignment with corporate goals. Then he had to find a way to continue to inspire that vision while working it through. He held himself and the entire team accountable instead of merely talking about it and demanding results at any cost.

Unfortunately, a common practice in business today is to get the job done at any cost. We know this comes all too often at the expensive of quality, health, morale, and job satisfaction, while breeding resentment and apathy. One of my primary roles in working with corporate executives is to teach them how to inspire results rather than dictate them. Communicating to inspire creates a positive, productive working environment.

The primary corporate communication technique I teach is simple but direct: always choose human eye-to-eye contact over e-mail or phone calls when a serious issue arises. This minimizes the confusion and misunderstandings that often arise from impersonal communications such as e-mails or voice mails. Nothing will ever replace the effectiveness and impact of one-to-one communication. And making the time to stop and go the extra step to reach out and clear lines of communication pays huge dividends. E-mails and phones are tools, but should never be relied upon to negotiate and redirect interpersonal challenges that require stopping, looking, and listening to the people involved.

The leader I worked with learned to interrupt his busy day and take the time to connect with team members. This provided him an additional opportunity to inspire the team by recasting the company's vision in person, while keeping the communication flowing. The team leader and members worked together for a year on these powerful techniques that produced a winning experience for all.

There are three perspectives to any business, organization or work environment that ensure a positive flow of communication and productivity. The first perspective, which I call the "I" perspective, refers to how each individual in the organization navigates stress.

Each member contributes to the second part of this dynamic, which I call the "We" perspective. This perspective refers to the various teams in the workplace, which are made up of individuals. Any work team can only be as healthy as the health of the individuals that make up the team. The team's collective approach to navigating communication and stress will either increase or decrease the team's productivity.

The third perspective, which I call the "It," refers to the organization as a whole. Every organization has the potential to be healthy or unhealthy in its unique connection to the marketplace, depending on the health of all the teams and the individuals comprising the organization.

One thing is certain: Just like an individual person, no organization (It) will ever consistently outperform the collective health or training of its teams (We), made up of individuals (I) that supply the organization's particular product or service. Awareness by everyone in the organization of the interrelationship between these three perspectives is vitally important to the overall success of the organization. It helps promote smooth operation, minimizes miscommunication and conflict, and enhances employee satisfaction and productivity.

# LEADING BY SERVING

Underlying the success of the *I – We – It* interrelationship is a commitment by everyone to the concept of servant leadership. That may sound like an oxymoron, but the philosophy of *servant leadership* is a rapidly growing perspective in the corporate world. More and more business leaders, executives and managers are discovering that servant leadership can actually enable their company to reach its highest potential of productivity and success.

Each individual in an organization must understand that the quickest way to the top is to focus on others' success before their own, knowing that their own success will come as they help others succeed. This concept has been the key to my own success and that of many others I have worked with.

Never underestimate the power and the dynamics that serving other people can bring to us. As we work to help others around us succeed, we end up helping ourselves become better at what we do, and better equipped to handle whatever lies down the road.

Some people try to explain away success by claiming that successful people simply got a lucky break. It's nothing of the sort. Once again, let me share my definition of luck: *preparation meeting opportunity*. Servant leaders prepare themselves for success by looking for opportunities to lift others up and help them succeed.

To be effective servant leaders, we need to understand, practice and apply the true meaning of the word "submit." To submit means to surrender oneself to something or someone else. This describes the characteristic of humility: relinquishing the illusion of internal control over external environments.

True submission, then, is a voluntary act that comes from a place of strength, not weakness. This quality is exemplified in the martial arts when opponents spar against each other in an exhibition or tournament, but bow to each other in respect at the beginning and end of each match. This simple gesture acknowledges that each opponent recognizes and respects the other's humanity, personality, unique individuality and dignity. This same quality of respect should characterize our relationships in the workplace.

Helping others in your organization succeed can be one of the most gratifying things you'll ever experience. When you help push others to the top, they pull you up along with them. The quickest way up the ladder of success is from the bottom up, helping others along the way and allowing them to pull you along with them.

This is the true definition of teamwork. Each individual strives to make each of the others better than any of them are alone. In doing so, the team moves forward together as one unit, helping the entire organization move forward.

Once this dynamic of servant leadership and teamwork is in place, and work teams see themselves and other teams succeeding as never before, individual members will begin to become aware of another powerful dynamic: gratitude.

Gratitude is one of the by-products of servant leadership in action. Expressing gratitude also happens to be one of the quickest ways to transition blood oxygen levels and therefore normalize stress. There are many situations to be grateful for in the workplace: for a level of company success previously considered unobtainable; for accelerating every team member to new heights of leadership, or for helping a teammate.

Remember, work stress comes in all forms, but the stress itself is not the issue. The real issue is converting that bad stress into a Good Stress experience to excel and grow while helping others around you do the same. Learning to communicate well and deal positively with people issues in the workplace is ultimately a very gratifying experience.

# ❥ *Good Stress In Action...*

Look at your workplace relationships. See where how you can convert negative stress to Good Stress. What can you do to effect this change? What preparation is needed? Lastly, find something to be grateful for in the current situation. Remember, the stress that you are feeling is a potential growth stimulus that can lead to elite performance.

# 9

# Relationship Stress

One of my most vivid memories of the Wat Yan Yao Temple mortuary is of an area simply called The Wall: a temporary wooden wall covered with photographs of hundreds of tsunami victims, each with an accompanying identification number.

Day after day I watched as distraught family members examined The Wall in hope or fear of identifying a missing loved one. Identifying the victims was no simple task. Rapidly advancing decomposition of the bodies made the identification process slow and painful. The sight of this daily procession of worried and grieving families searching desperately to determine the fate of their loved ones often brought tears to my eyes. I was reminded yet again of how the tsunami was a force unlike any seen before in modern history with the possible exception of the nuclear bomb.

I met one gentleman who had flown to Thailand from his home in Germany to locate a missing relative. Three days of fruitless searching yielded no match for the picture he had brought with him, leaving this poor man frustrated and despondent. Even the separation of Thai victims from international victims for easier identification did not help him. Sadly and reluctantly, he returned to Germany with picture in hand, but no body to take home for burial.

Stress in this tsunami-ravaged area of the world came in many different forms. Processing it daily and helping others to do the same thing was a normal day for me in Khao Lak. Relational stress was particularly acute for the thousands of friends and families whose relationships with the victims had been so suddenly and violently severed. This brought to light the importance of connectedness in human society.

# THE POWER OF CONNECTEDNESS

Understanding the awesome power of our connectedness to one another is vital to living a satisfyingly full life. Our modern, high-tech world of Internet, GPS, cell phones, text messaging, and digital, fiber-optic and wireless telecommunications makes us the most connected generation in history, and on a truly global scale. Yet ironically we human beings are perhaps even less sincerely connected with each other than at any other time in history.

With the click of a mouse we can access millions of bits of information electronically. We no longer need to interact directly with another person to get the information we seek. This technological capability has had the effect of isolating us from each other more and more. As technology expands our global village, our emotional distance also increases. Nevertheless, with six billion of us sharing the same small planet – are all on a journey through life together.

Whatever our race, nation or culture, we all share the inborn need to love and be loved, to connect and relate to other people. The poet John Donne wrote, "No man is an island, entire of itself; every man is a piece of the continent, a part of the main." Paul of Tarsus, one of the New Testament writers, said, "For none of us lives to himself, and no one dies to himself" (Rom. 14:7).

Everything we say and do affects other people because we are all interconnected in the same space/time continuum, living lives that intersect daily with those of family, friends and colleagues. There is incredible power in this concept of our shared connectedness that can dramatically increase our ability to cope with frustrating and potentially harmful situations.

As we each embrace our connectedness with everyone in our global village, we are making our world a better place in which to live and belong. One key secret to living younger longer is understanding and accepting our connectedness to others. In truth, we are really not that different after all.

The best way to instill this understanding throughout the world is teaching it to young children before the ego takes hold. Understanding our connectedness to others around the world can help us live fulfilling lives.

# A SERVANT'S HEART – THE KEY TO RELATIONAL SUCCESS

As I discussed earlier, the principles of effective corporate communication are to connect, to influence and to lead. The most effective leaders practice servant leadership, approaching their responsibility with a humble spirit. Unfortunately, many people clamor after success believing that the only way is to claw their way to the top, climbing over or shoving aside any who stand in their way. The higher they rise the more they think they are entitled to be served. They are not aware that there is a healthy path to success.

A servant attitude is key to effective communication both at home and at work. A servant mentality goes a long way in helping us connect with someone else and stay connected, because everyone desires to be served. This is especially true in the service-oriented world that we live in today.

Servant-hearted people seek to treat everyone with equanimity no matter how pleasant or unpleasant they are or how deserving or undeserving they may be. I understand quite well how difficult working with the public can be sometimes. But as difficult as it may be to execute, everyone is entitled to quality service and respect. Servant-hearted individuals understand this and do not feel threatened by obnoxious or unpleasant people. Their emotional stability and self-esteem do not depend on the approval of others.

A service mindset is always appropriate. A servant attitude on the giving side goes a long way toward drawing a reciprocal response from the receiving side. It's the Golden Rule in action: Treat others as you wish to be treated.

Another characteristic of a servant attitude focused on effective communication is never to assume that others understand what we say and what we mean. Sometimes we can get so lost in our own thoughts and agendas that we act as though we expect everybody to read our minds. We think they should know our looks, gestures, quirks and silly ways because after all, most days are all about us. Right?

When it comes to miscommunication and relational problems at home or at work, the causative factor is often the lack of proper training and implementation of a servant attitude. If two people in either a work or domestic relationship are committed to serving each other, both will have their needs met more often than not.

Interesting enough, the Greek word genes means to ingest or impregnate, and this is where we get our English word *know*. So to know someone or something is to understand it with emotion, conviction, and passion. Inspiration is the power source God created to help us procreate through language, art, dance and music. This powerful force also inspires great human relationships and creates motivation, passion and perseverance.

# Dating Dynamics

Teenage years can be especially stressful because young people are busy trying their wings and forging their own identities. This commonly brings them into stress and conflict with parents, siblings and others. Add to that the stress of dating and it's easy to understand why the teen years can be so tough.

Dating is a courtship ritual filled with stress but also with excitement, which is inherently Good Stress. This is true whether the persons involved are teenagers just entering the dating world, or divorced or widowed people re-entering the dating field.

Do you remember your first date? Perhaps you went to the school prom or on a double date with another couple. Do you remember how you got all dressed up and wanted to impress your date with your charm and grace? Do you remember how nervous and awkward you felt? How did your first date turn out? Did the two of you hit it off well and discover that you had a lot in common? Or were you like oil and water, mismatched and uncomfortable, wishing and waiting anxiously for the evening to end? And what about later dates, either with the same person or with someone else? Maybe you got lucky and hooked up with someone you really liked, only to find out later that your new flame was interested only in a good time and nothing else.

Dating life is a mixed bag of positive and negative experiences. Depending on how we respond to those experiences and what we learn from them, we can set ourselves up for either a lifetime of satisfaction or a lifetime of disappointment and negative relationship stress.

It's human nature to make mistakes in relationships, but unless we learn from them we suffer a lifelong pattern of inappropriate choices. The stress management principles are the same here as for dealing with any other kind of stress. Unfortunately, many people either do not know the principles or do not understand how to apply them in their relationships.

A key to successful dating and a successful marriage is first to become completely comfortable being single. Some people who grow up in negative or destructive home environments can't wait to escape. They jump into the first reasonable-looking relationship that comes along, even though they have underdeveloped self-esteem and little sense of self-identity. The psychological and emotional stress of not really knowing who they are, coupled with the natural stresses that come with any developing relationship, sets these folks up for disappointment and probably a failed relationship.

Being single has many advantages. Your life is your own. You have only your own schedule to consider, and fewer compromises to make regarding what you do and when you do it. You can leave your house or apartment as neat or as messy as you desire. You can live your life with no complicating long-term relational obligations or commitments to anyone except immediate family members.

Some people prefer the single life, finding it a quiet and safe place to live and grow. Their temperament and life and career goals seem suited to the single life. Others are miserable in that single state and consider it a very temporary phase of life. When the right person comes along, they will leave singleness behind without hesitation or regret.

Whether you are single and satisfied, single and dating or single and eagerly waiting to meet the right person, the key to contentment is learning how to make the most of your life and circumstances right now. It's fine to have dreams, as long as they don't make you miserable in the present. I have stated before that 90% of reality is perception, which can be changed, while the other 10% is as unchangeable as gravity and must be accepted.

Perception makes all the difference. I have found that mental and verbal affirmations can be very empowering and comforting no matter what our life situation. Here is one that works well in any circumstance: *Whatever situation you are in today, be all there and look for the good in everything.* If you are single, enjoy that freedom and self-expression until someone steps into your world to change that reality. Having this mindset can change the internal pressure of the urgency of finding a partner into a calm and peaceful space where you can flourish, grow and bloom where you are currently planted.

Perhaps you are single and dating and are anxious to be plucked up from your present garden and replanted in someone else's. Don't be in a big hurry. The time may not be right. You may not be ready yet for a transplant. Use this time to weed out your own garden space to help you be ready to fully appreciate and enjoy your next transition.

Don't expect anybody to walk into your life and change it for the better without any work or growth on your part. Life doesn't work that way. Take every opportunity right now to become a confident, satisfied, self-fulfilled single who isn't looking for fulfillment or completion through another person, who knows how to process stress in his or her own life and turn it into a positive catalyst. This is preparing for relationship success. When you do this successfully with yourself first, you have a much better chance of doing it with another person. This is the process of creating your own "luck." Be ready when that right person comes along, and you'll be ready to enter a strong, positive, fruitful and lasting relationship. This is preparation meeting opportunity.

# THE MARRIAGE MAZE

The strongest marriage occurs between two people who are comfortable and secure within themselves first. This is a critical key to successful marriage that is too often overlooked or completely ignored. If we are not comfortable with who we are, how can we expect to get along well with someone else in a day-to-day intimate relationship? If we have a low self-image or an incomplete sense of personal identity, we will end up consciously or unconsciously trying to control or manipulate the other person into meeting our needs. That person then becomes a commodity to be used rather than a partner to be loved and cherished. Understanding this simple dynamic is critical to maintaining any healthy and vibrant relationship, especially marriage.

Marriage is a two-way street that two people must travel together. Success on this journey requires the deepest level of commitment and shared understanding. It also requires clear, open and honest channels of communication about everything from emotions and needs to finances and children.

I have counseled many married couples who did not realize the importance of clear and effective communication. Communication is to a marriage like oxygen is to life; it keeps everything alive. In marriage, everything begins and ends with communication.

Most extramarital affairs take place not because of unmet physical or sexual needs but because of poor communication, which often leads to unfulfilled emotional needs. Married people enter affairs in an effort to find someone they can communicate with, someone who will share their interests and simply listen to them.

Marriage is a union of two people who willingly give their lives for each other with a willingness to commit to and serve each other daily. It is a partnership with mutually agreed upon ground rules, shared values and a willingness to stick it out through thick and thin, working through all challenges together.

Part of this process is a mutual commitment to keep looking forward because success lies ahead, not behind. One of the quickest ways to disrupt a healthy relationship is by dwelling on the past. Reflecting on the past to learn and grow is one thing, but reverting to past failures and flaws only produces pain, insecurity, and fear of failure. Most people will endure only a certain amount of pain before they look around for relief.

The difference between a wound and a scar is the pain. A wound is open, raw, bleeding and painful with the risk of a dangerous infection. A scar is the sign of healing that shows where the wound once was. Once healing is complete, there is no pain, only the memory of pain.

Hurt in a relationship is like an open, bleeding wound: painful and raw. Forgiveness, on the other hand, is like a scar. Healing has come and pain has gone but a life has been changed forever in a greater or subtler way. Wounds inflict pain but scars build character. They are the evidence of experience gained, lessons learned and life storms weathered.

No matter how happy and successful a marriage may be, it can sometimes benefit from some advanced training or counsel along the way. If your marital journey becomes mired with roadblocks and obstacles, consider seeking professional coaching to learn new attitudes and behaviors to increase your overall relational success.

# ✦ *Good Stress In Action...*

Find a way to be of service to your partner or another person today. Anything will do: a smile or a kind word, taking time out to help someone, donating some money to your favorite charity. Small positive actions make a big difference. We are all related either by blood, association or humanity and have a common need to share space, time, energy and knowledge. Since we are all sharing this same planet as we journey through life, wouldn't it be better to serve as many people as possible along the way, thus finding a deeper and more meaningful life experience?

# Parenting Stress

Thailand was only one of many Asian and Pacific nations affected by the December 26, 2004 tsunami disaster. More than 175,000 people died in that short 40 minutes, nearly 130,000 in Indonesia alone. Although international financial and material assistance to the stricken nations came quickly and abundantly, Thailand seemed to be near the bottom of the list in receiving such aid because it had far fewer casualties than the other nations. In fact, there were no US medical teams in Thailand; they were relegated to other areas. Yet in terms of property and industry Thailand was just as devastated as the other countries.

Everyone I encountered in the Phuket/Pang Nag province of southern Thailand knew at least one person who had been lost or injured in the tragedy. In the end, I extended my stay in Thailand for two weeks out of solidarity. Very little

U.S. assistance was available and few American volunteers were on site. I felt it was important for me to stay there to represent my work and my country.

Thailand is a beautiful country of teak forests, lush green mountains, undulating rice paddies and gilded Buddhist temples, long stretches of pristine beaches and birds of every imaginable color, but it is the generous character of Thai people that makes the country so remarkable. The Thai sense of fun, concern for the well-being of others, grace and decorum, and most of all, the deep gratitude towards outsiders assisting them were evident everywhere. It is the custom of Thai people to treat everyone – especially visitors – like family. That is certainly the regard that was extended to me by everyone I met.

Such widespread politeness and respect do not develop overnight or by accident. In Thailand these qualities are taught to children from birth and encouraged at every level of the society. Thailand is a predominantly Buddhist nation of the Theravada orthodoxy, the sect of Buddhism closest to the Buddha's teachings. It is quite socially and culturally different from America. For one thing, the Thai people take family and parenting responsibilities very seriously.

# PARENTING: THE GREAT ADVENTURE

If you are looking for adventure in your life, become a parent! You'll find yourself on the fast track so quickly it'll make your head spin. Nothing will show you the meaning of "energy" faster than keeping up with a two-year-old for half an hour – endless running, jumping, climbing and countless questions. No wonder so many parents have so little energy left at the end of the day. As wonderful as they are, children inject stress into a home and a marriage. This is why applying the principles of good stress is as important for parents as for anyone else.

Parenting stress comes in all shapes, sizes and colors. Children thrill us and frighten us, make us happy and sad, fill us with pride and with disappointment. All of these things can be stressful, but remember: Positive or negative, stress is stress and parents need to know how to process it successfully. If more parents knew how to do this, there would be less domestic violence, less child abuse, less divorce and fewer troubled kids.

Speaking as a parent, I will be the first to say that children are a blessing. One of the greatest joys in life is to have children and help them grow into healthy, well-adjusted and responsible adults. All parents have their own unique stories and memories of raising their children. Over the past twenty years I have had the privilege of raising two boys and there have been plenty of challenging days and long nights, especially with Brandon, my special-needs son.

Raising Brandon has been my greatest personal challenge and joy. Learning to be a father to a child who needs 24/7 care to eat, move, sleep and bathe and be entertained during waking hours has matured me in every dimension of my life. It made me a better man and a better husband. Brandon's love of life in spite of his enormous challenges inspires me to live my life to the fullest every day and find purpose and fulfillment in empowering others. Taking care of him has taught me the greatest truths about the potential of stress as a positive force.

First-time parents learn quickly how demanding, rewarding and draining this awesome job of parenting can be. Even though our children grow up, move out and start lives, careers and families of their own, and the situations and dynamics of our relationships with them change, they will always be our children.

The preparation and anticipation of a new arrival into a home – particularly the first one – is just the beginning of the necessary steps and attitudes that new parents will develop over the next eighteen years. From the moment a child is brought into the world, nothing is ever going to be the same again for the parents. Their view of the world is altered by their responsibility for this precious new life that is growing and learning under their watchful care.

Many new parents protect their first child like a priceless but fragile Ming vase with regard to everything from eating, bathing and car seats to the overall safety of the entire home. After learning with the first child, they realize that they can relax a little with the second and any subsequent children.

Raising a child is the best form of adult therapy available anywhere on the planet because of all the self-actualization that takes place as parents observe their children. Watching our children grow and develop is like looking into a mirror: we see the good, the bad and the ugly from our own childhood in the character and personality of our children.

To one extent or another, we all act out of our own childhood experiences. Breaking any negative conditionings from the past requires a new training with new knowledge to create a new dynamic of confidence, strength and hope. This will help ensure a better future for our children.

Two seemingly contradictory characteristics that make for good parenting and alleviating parenting stress are humility and confidence. Parenting with humility requires compassionate remembering of what it was like to be a child growing up. This helps us to empathize with our children. Parenting from a place of confidence means being secure within ourselves so that we feel no need to prove anything to our children. Being confident of ourselves and our authority helps us avoid the temptation of going too far with a disciplinary action, or of making empty threats that our children know we don't mean.

Parents who lack confidence often overcompensate by becoming excessively demanding or controlling of their children. Some insecure parents take the opposite tack of abdicating their responsibility, essentially abandoning their children to make up their own rules and establish their own boundaries. Either extreme may create children who are estranged from their parents, contemptuous of authority and confused about right and wrong.

# THREE PARENTING DYNAMICS

Ideal parenting involves molding and shaping a child into an honest, morally upright and productive adult of high character and integrity. Parents have a tough job, and the demands and expectations of modern society don't make it any easier. Whether parenting as a married couple, single or blended family, parenting dynamics are essentially the same.

Whether the parents are a couple parenting their own biological children, are single parents, or creating a blended family, parenting stress is parenting stress. Parents can transform this stress into a positive energy that inspires them to excellence in all areas of life and provides them with many opportunities for positive teaching, including reinforcing key values and influencing healthy behaviors.

Many parents keep repeating the same mistakes with their children because they don't know how to change. Most of us parent the way we were parented. Even if we recognize our weaknesses and want to do things differently, when the going gets tough we tend to revert back to what we saw growing up.

How can parents adopt positive alternatives? The answer is training. I'm not talking about in-depth parenting classes or counseling, although many of those programs can be very helpful. I'm talking about the basic common-sense principles for stress management.

Of the three parenting dynamics that we see today, the blended family is becoming more prevalent. The children in a blended family sometimes have anger, hurt, grief and/or guilt issues that make it difficult for them to respect the authority of the stepparent. Parents in this situation need to be sensitive to the children's needs and tread extremely carefully.

In a blended family situation, the biological parent is usually the heavy when it comes to carrying out discipline, and the stepparent serves a supporting role. This approach accomplishes two things: First, it minimizes resentment on the part of children who may not accept discipline coming primarily from a stepparent. Second, it helps assure that both parents convey a message that is clear, concise and consistent to the children.

# COMMUNICATE CLEARLY

As with workplace and relationship stress, one of the key elements for navigating parenting stress is developing and maintaining clear lines of communication. Children are masters at playing one parent against the other. This is especially true of a strong-willed child. The child tries to wheedle one parent and if that fails goes to the other one. Unless the parents have their act together in communicating a clear, consistent and mutually supportive message, this scenario can degenerate into a he-said/she-said match that nobody wins.

Clear communication between parents is essential: Clear parent/child communication is just as important. Nothing confuses and unsettles children faster than inconsistency in parenting. Sending mixed messages, saying yes one time and no the next, arbitrary punishment, empty threats, hollow promises and inconsistent boundaries leave children feeling fearful and insecure. They don't know who to believe or what to depend on.

Clear communication to children also means modeling the behavior we want them to adopt. The old saying, "Do as I say, not as I do," rarely works in implementation. Children are natural-born mimics; it's how they learn. They will imitate what we do and say regardless of how we tell them to behave.

All of us learn our behavior primarily through observing others. Actions really do speak louder than words, especially to children. They need healthy, consistent role models to set their lives on solid tracks for success.

## *DISCIPLINE CONSISTENTLY AND FAIRLY IN LOVE*

The most important way to model success for our children is to relate to them clearly and consistently with unconditional love. Unconditional doesn't mean "I'll love you *if...*" or "I'll love you *when...*" It means "I love you...*period.*" Children need to know that they are loved unconditionally – that nothing they say or do will ever destroy or change their parents' love for them.

Consistent and fair discipline is the greatest act of love that parents can give to their children. Properly administered, discipline corrects wrong behavior, rewards right behavior and teaches our children how to make proper decisions and choices in life consistently. Good discipline can also train them how to think and act consistently under pressure, in a manner that produces the most beneficial results.

Developing consistent behavior under pressure is why military training places such an emphasis on discipline. In a crisis situation like combat, good training will override emotion so that soldiers make the right decisions to accomplish the mission and stay alive in the process.

Parental discipline instills in children the beliefs, values and principles that will help them choose the right path for excellence and success, regardless of their stress level. Children who are trained with fair and consistent discipline are much less likely to compromise their values, character or integrity later in life when the crunch comes.

The basic morals and values that are deeply planted inside each of us must also be internalized by our children so that they will understand as they grow up that there is a point of reference for every decision they make. We rise or fall – and sometimes live or die – by our decisions. The earlier in life our children learn to make decisions from a place of balance and healthiness, the better their decision-making process will be later in life.

As I said earlier, one key to successful parenting is remembering what it was like to be a child. It is vitally important to remain "real" about the ups and downs involved in a child's maturation process. Many were the times I could see my own past behavior coming out in one of my boys, and it was always a very difficult thing for me to handle. Remembering what it was like growing up can keep us from overreacting so that we don't administer discipline in the heat of anger when one of our kids acts out.

Disciplining from a place of anger is unhealthy for both child and parent. Anger is a toxic emotion that must be processed before administering discipline or our response may be too harsh. Discipline administered out of anger is not discipline: It is punishment or, even worse, abuse. Disciplining in anger is one of the primary causes of physical child abuse. This is why approaching the parenting role from a framework of mastery over stress provides a tremendous advantage. When you prepare properly, process well and allow time for rest, recovery and debriefing there is a significantly greater chance that negative emotions will not permeate your relationships. You will understand that through breathing you can transmute the anger which will preserve the unconditional love that is so critically important in all relationships. Unconditional love is really just another form of the Golden Rule: loving others, especially our children, the way we want to be loved.

Many parents have brought their children to me for counseling and asked me to "fix them." I tell the parents that I need several sessions with them before treating their child because often many of the children's problems stem from the dynamics of the parents' parenting style and motivation.

Often the behavior of the child I am supposed to "fix" improves dramatically after I train the parents with some basic tools to help them transform the entire dynamic of their home environment. Some parents shy away from administering discipline out of fear that it is unfair and potentially damaging to a child's fragile psyche. Parents who feel this way misunderstand the purpose of discipline – training and correction.

The word discipline is a variation of the word disciple, which means "student" or "learner." A disciple is a person who studies under the tutelage of a master teacher or mentor. Discipline is designed to train children how to live, how to act, how to think independently and how to make sound decisions. Properly administered, discipline is an act of love. Love does not let a child remain in ignorance. Love does not let a child continue in wrong or self-destructive behavior. Love does not allow children to make decisions and choices they are not mature enough to make.

Love teaches a child self-respect. Love teaches a child to respect the rights, feelings, property and life of others. Love teaches a child to respect legitimate authority. Love teaches a child social skills. Love is always available to a child and makes sure the child knows it.

Young children are more receptive to correction than teenagers because they are eager to be loved, and they will know they are loved if that discipline is administered fairly and consistently in love. Teens also need love, affection and attention but in different ways than young children. Teens often want to know that the environment is safe for them to explore and learn on their own. Since the teen years are training for adulthood, it is always helpful for parents to remember their own passage through this *often difficult* time. And remember, they will move through it to the other side, but at their own pace. Honoring this fundamental difference is often enough to restore peace to an otherwise challenging parent/child dynamic. Reassuring them that you are there and leading by example are excellent ways to manage stress levels.

# ESTABLISH APPROPRIATE AND REASONABLE BOUNDARIES

Gang wars and school shootings happen because no one is watching closely enough to discipline those children through love, in order to correct their undesirable and antisocial behavior. All children crave acceptance. If they don't find it through the traditional avenues of family, friends, religious affiliation or community groups or clubs, they will seek it in disruptive, reckless or even self-destructive behavior. Furthermore, where there is poverty (especially financial, but also emotional and spiritual), there is crime and rebellion.

Many kids, frustrated in their efforts to find acceptance, become angry and bitter and rebel by turning to crime or violence. Many of the ADD/ADHD-diagnosed young people are actually kids who are growing up without healthy boundaries and discipline. Kids will try to fit in with others, either through acceptance or through disruption, violence, and corruption. Many of the young people I treated who were struggling in school fell into the oppositional defiant disorder instead of the distractibility category simply because of a lack of boundaries and discipline. Their distractibility was not due to a chemical deficiency. It was a symptom of their need to fit in. Because of the lack of discipline at home, they tried forcing their ways upon others.

Of course many people do struggle with Attention Defect Disorder including Hyperactivity (ADD/ADHD) that is caused by an imbalance in brain chemistry. This is often due to poor food choices rather than environment. In these cases medication may be helpful when used and monitored carefully. But I believe that far too many children are being medicated as a quick fix for behavioral problems when the real culprit is the lack of discipline and clear boundaries at home. These boundaries include guidelines for television, computer and cell-phone use, as well as overall behavior. Unless the real problem is addressed, these troubled kids will grow into troubled adults and will have problems all their lives.

Much parenting stress stems from an inadequate understanding of the parents' own motivations and deepest longings. Insecure and unfulfilled parents project their negativities on their children, perpetuating a cycle of broken lives, shattered dreams and poor self-esteem that cultivate the entitlement mentality or learned helplessness so pervasive in today's society.

It is reassuring to know that consistent, fair and loving discipline coupled with reasonable and age-appropriate boundaries is a formula for raising healthy, confident, secure and well-adjusted children who grow into happy and productive adults.

# ✦ *Good Stress In Action...*

Use the stresses of the family dynamic to teach your children the importance of self-responsibility. Making good parenting an integral part of your life's purpose has tremendous value to all. Reflect on your family dynamic today, remembering your own childhood, and choose an area in which you would like to affect some change. Pay close attention to the daily details of this issue and determine where additional discipline, training and strategy could produce a more desirable outcome. Work with the stress preparation model that you have learned to plan for and make the change, and then lean into the success that you want to see.

# The Stress of Divorce

Returning to Bangkok after three weeks in Thailand's disaster zone, it was strange to be in a cosmopolitan city where residents and visitors alike carried on business as usual, while only a hundred miles to the south people were trying to survive shattered lives and conditions. Bangkok's bustling streets looked almost normal, if you consider rivers of pedicabs, bicycles, cars, trucks, buses – and padi boats on the Chao Praya River, enveloped by an incredible thick heat haze – normal. I found it hard to believe that it was only an hour by air from Phuket, where the tsunami had wiped out villages and human lives in a holiday season that was supposed to be so merry.

I do regular interviews for TV and radio in the US and am commonly asked, "How do you handle the stress of caring for so many hurting people?" My response is, "Stress is not the problem. The real problem is not taking sufficient breaks to refresh and recover throughout the long draining days." Plus, I feel rewarded by my work; it is inspiring to see people raise themselves to higher and higher levels of being and understanding.

# NO ONE "PLANS" TO DIVORCE

Aside from the death of a loved one, divorce is probably the most common grief-causing event in life because it represents the death of a marriage relationship. Divorce is never in the minds of the couple standing at the altar waiting to say "I do." But the truth is that no couple is completely immune from the danger. Even the most loving and committed couple can sometimes be blindsided by an event so traumatic or devastating – the sudden death of a child, for example – that their marriage does not survive the aftermath.

The likelihood of divorce in such a situation, or any other situation, can be greatly mitigated when couples apply the concepts of Good Stress *before* marital problems begin. But even if divorce looms as a reality before them, applying the principles of Good Stress can minimize the emotional damage for everyone involved and allow the couple a smooth transition with as few bumps as possible.

A significant part of the divorce problem in America stems from the fact that many couples in the throes of love get married before taking the time to truly know either themselves or each other, or to carefully consider the responsibilities of marriage. They assume that love alone will keep them together. Nothing could ever intervene in their intention to live the rest of their lives with each other. But as many of us learn, love alone is not enough. Marital success requires love, lots of hard work and the commitment to truth, honesty and openness in communications. Success in love and marriage never comes accidentally or overnight. It must be carefully planned for and diligently worked for.

Love is tricky to navigate even in the best of circumstances. One step toward future success is for each person to look deep within and identify his or her personal hopes, dreams, expectations and understanding of love and marriage. This can be the beginning of an empowering journey of self-awareness and self-discovery that truly prepares one for a lifelong relationship with a significant other.

Love is more than a feeling or emotion; it's a way of being. Love is a choice, a commitment that is filled with all the uncertainty of future dreams and aspirations. Love is a vibrant, living and growing state of mental, emotional, spiritual and physical equilibrium that must be balanced and maintained daily. We all know how stressful love can be. Anyone who has ever sat at the bedside of a critically ill spouse or child knows just how stressful. Sometimes it seems as though it would be easier not to love because then there is less risk of pain and heartache. But not loving is not an option, because we all need to love and be loved.

Do you remember when you were young, free, and full of hope and expectations for a great future? Maybe you still are. The thrill of the pursuit; the dance of dating and courtship; the fear of rejection; the ecstasy of winning the object of your love; all of this is a natural phase of life and development. Just as natural is the reality that these dynamics change and mature over time and if you don't keep attuned to them, your relationship may falter.

Divorce may loom on the horizon when a couple's rules, beliefs and dreams change with age and responsibility, yet one or the other or both are unwilling to change accordingly. Change is healthy and resisting change is stagnation. Sometimes, however, both parties are changing but in different directions. In such cases, divorce can be quite healthy. If the two people are mature and conscious, their relationship can take another form such as friendship and continue to flourish. It's important to realize that relationships really never end, they simply take a different form – especially when we've had many years with a person. When we are open to learning from divorce and embracing the positive aspects of it, we will manage the stress of it as successfully as we manage stress in other areas of our life.

In other relationships, as tension mounts and dissatisfaction grows, divorce becomes an option for escape. Certainly the likelihood of divorce increases if one party chafes under marital or familial problems, while the other party continues to move through daily life in denial of the domestic challenges. How two people in the relationship handle stress overall is one factor that determines their long-term viability as a married couple.

# GRIEF IS STRESS

All divorcing couples must traverse the rocky landscape of grief before coming to rest on smooth ground again. This takes time, understanding, patience and the belief that life will return to some form of normal, however we define this for ourselves. With divorce, as any other loss, we must transition from a past reality to a new future reality.

Understanding the grief process and potential choke points that can lock individuals out of a healthy recovery process are the keys to helping traumatized people rebuild their lives. The key to understanding the grief process and its challenges begins with remembering our own grief experiences. What have we learned from those experiences? How can we apply those lessons to the current circumstances?

Divorce is a painful tearing away that must be navigated properly in order to avoid sustained grief, sorrow, anger, bitterness and regret that may carry on into future relationships. The pain of this tearing-away process is what we call grief, and it can be just as intense for people going through divorce as it is for people experiencing the death of a loved one. Simply stated, grief is the transition between past reality and future reality. This desert place can be so painful that for much of the time death may seem like the only relief in sight. Grief can shut down and cripple even the strongest of individuals. Although it is an unbearable emotion, it is also temporary. Learning to view grief as a transitional period during which growth, healing and evolution occur, however, can encourage and inspire us and carry us through the darkest days because we know that transition is temporary.

It is only natural that grief carries a great deal of pain and sorrow but it can become unhealthy and even deadly for anyone who fails to process it correctly. As with the fight or flight hormones that aid the body in self-defense but are toxic in large amounts, grief is also toxic if prolonged.

I often tell people that I am a professional griever: I have been grieving for two decades over the illness of my son. My grief is not toxic grief however, because I have learned to process and work with it regularly, and have experienced so many positive things through the grieving. My sadness over Brandon's condition has dramatically affected my view of life, reality and the world. I once believed that grief was something that only took place when we lost someone in death, but I now understand that grief can occur over losses of all kinds, like of that of a job, or loss of a relationship. One can even experience grief during positive changes such as moving, marriage or having children, because we are leaving something behind in exchange for something new.

Grief is a cathartic process that flushes toxic energy and emotions from our system. Were these toxins to remain, they could cause disease, constant chronic fatigue, confusion, and possibly shorten our life expectancy. The grief process follows an ebb and flow from the moment of injury to the moment of full recovery. This process is usually so consistent that it can be charted to help us navigate through this painful period.

Grief normally progresses through several stages of varying duration, depending on the nature of the grief and the emotional makeup of the griever:

• Shock — a defense mechanism that isolates us emotionally from the full implications of the loss. Denial commonly appears in this stage.

• Catharsis — the stage where most of the emotional venting takes place, resulting in a significant release of physical and emotional tension.

• Depression — a common occurrence as the full reality of the loss settles in and recognition comes as to how much things have truly changed because of the loss.

• Guilt — self-recrimination when the griever fears or imagines that he or she bears direct or significant responsibility for the loss, i.e. "I should have done more…"

• Loss Preoccupation — fixation on the loss itself and the what-ifs of how it could have been avoided.

• Anger — lashing out at God or at the unfairness of life, or even at the person who has died or is otherwise the object of the loss. This is a final cathartic step that clears the way for a return to normalcy.

• Reality Adaptation — recognizing and accepting the new reality that exists after the loss. Those who reach this stage have made the transition and are ready to resume normal life.

This natural grief process allows us to navigate through intense pain and survive a painful loss without self-destructing. Normally, the process can last several months or longer and usually flows back and forth between the stages. It is always helpful to have professional help during a grieving process. Eventually, however, the elapsed time in each progressive stage will decrease, signaling that relief and normalcy are just around the corner.

Sometimes prolonging one of these stages can cause tremendous pain and destruction to oneself and others around the person. Getting stuck in a stage may require professional treatment. For example, in the case of divorce a person may begin the grieving process and get stuck in the anger stage. Until the anger is properly resolved, the person will not be able to move on to the reality adaptation stage. Someone stuck in anger will see the world only through the lenses of regret and hostility, and have little positive to say about anyone of the opposite sex. They may even become bashers of anyone who is trying to have a healthy and growing relationship.

An admiral who trained Navy SEALS once told me that pain is negative energy leaving the body. If you know anything about the training regimen of Navy SEALS, then you can see that this admiral knows a thing or two about pain. Living through pain produces a potential learning experience that can positively influence future life decisions. I agree with his assessment. I believe that pain processed correctly yields great growth and learning opportunity that can prepare us for any crisis.

Remember that pain is not the same as injury. Pain can be the stimulus for growth while injury, if not protected, can cause more destructive pain and increased injury. If we can train ourselves to differentiate between pain and injury, then pushing through our pain to the other side will give us a whole new understanding of our limits, our capabilities and ourselves.

# LOSING GRANDMA BLICK

Life has interesting ways of teaching us how to cope with negative circumstances and to make us grow strong as a result. I lost two of my grandparents when I was growing up, one when I was 13 and the other when I was 14. Early on I learned that the loss of a loved one is something that must be navigated, not just endured.

Loss is never easy in any shape or form, but it can teach us how to live and how to hold onto the tangible things in life that really mean the most to us. Losing two grandparents at a young age taught me the valuable lesson of always looking ahead at what life can be, instead of just looking around at life only as it is at the moment.

When I was a young adult I lost a third grandparent, my maternal grandmother. Grandma Blick was a wonderful woman who had a profound influence on my young life. For many years I spent every summer with her and my grandfather in the middle of nowhere in southern Kentucky. Their house was so deep in the woods that they used to joke about piping sunlight in every day so that we could work in its presence. My summers with them taught me that even though life may involve a lot of hard work, it is something to be enjoyed every day.

We would awake early, eat a hearty breakfast and go to the field to work, carrying our lunches in brown bags. I learned a lot from Grandma and Grandpa Blick because I was older at the time and knew what questions to ask and also how to learn by observing their behavior. Grandma Blick used to tell me that greatness was deep inside of me. She encouraged me to pursue every possibility for my life. She dreamed great dreams for me and instilled them in my heart even though her own life appeared to be somewhat lacking in excitement, stowed away as she was on a farm in the middle of nowhere.

One summer on my "working" vacation, my favorite dog passed away of old age. No one was around except Grandma Blick. This was the first significant loss of my life, and it became my responsibility to bury my dear collie in a field behind the house.

I remember the horrible weight of the burlap sack, dragging it down the road. After digging a hole, Grandma and I performing a small funeral service. Then I put his body in the hole, covered it up with dirt and tried to control my tears. That loss cut very deeply in me as a 12-year-old. It affected my sleep cycle for a while. I would wake in the night wishing that my dog were still around.

Even today, when I see a collie I think of that dog of mine. I remember the fun we had together. And I think of that day I dragged my old buddy down the road in that burlap bag and consigned his body to the ground with my own hands. I still remember how alone I felt in my grief. This was my first experience of grief, yet something inside told me that I would need to move on.

Years later when I was living in Anchorage, Alaska, attending school and working at Elmendorf Air Force Base, working hard and trying to raise a young family on a modest income, I got the news that Grandma Blick had passed away. Again, I felt the grief of losing someone close to me. Living through the transition of that grief and loss was tough. Yet over time it also yielded a treasured opportunity to reflect on the life lessons that Grandma Blick taught me – life lessons that have greatly shaped the man I am today.

I lost my father in the early-idea stage of this book, which also has had a profound impact on my life. He was a quiet but intentional man with a strong work ethic and a love for children like no one I have ever known. He loved my boys deeply and had a very special love for Brandon. I think he related to Brandon's disabilities, having himself survived three strokes, plus weeks of therapy learning how to walk and speak again after each stroke, before finally passing away of heart failure. Losing anyone close to us can leave an indelible mark of pain and cause us to examine our destiny. When I spoke at my dad's funeral, I was able to share stories about how much he loved people and life in general. I remember looking into the crowd and seeing Brandon looking back at me, not yet understanding that his grandpa and dear friend would never again be able to push him around in his wheelchair and laugh out loud while crashing into walls and door frames. In that moment, my composure dissolved. I struggled to stay focused on my thoughts through the tears – tears of joy for having had a father like him to remember and tears of pain for losing him. I have fond memories of my dad and look forward to someday visiting with him in another world and saying all the things we neglected to discuss when he was here. So remember to connect to those who are significant to you *today,* because, like my dad's passing, loss can come without warning and with no second chance to say goodbye.

# Stay and Learn? Or Leave and Learn?

Like the death of a loved one, divorce ignites the grief process because divorce signals the death of a marriage. Grief is grief, just as stress is stress, and although the object of grief may change, the stages of the process and the pain of loss endured are the same.

Couples going through a divorce experience deep and wrenching pain that is sometimes made even worse by the public nature of that pain. But no matter how painful and traumatic divorce may be for the husband and wife, it is worse for their children.

Essentially there are two ways to respond to life in general and divorce in particular: reactively and proactively. With a reactive approach, people with little or no training, preparation, goal or sense of purpose, simply react to whatever life throws at them. They bounce from one crisis to another like a pinball. Reactive people frequently attract the same problems and relive the same difficulties over and again, because they have not learned from their past experiences and mistakes.

Proactive people, on the other hand, look at life with its ups and downs as a great classroom for growth and learning. They approach life head-on, falling forward. They regard even their mistakes and bad experiences as learning opportunities. Proactive people know that even negative events and circumstances can be changed into rocket fuel to propel them to excellence in performance and fully realized potential. Proactive people understand the principles of Good Stress.

This is critical when it comes to navigating the choppy waters and sharp rocks of divorce. I have counseled numerous individuals and couples who were looking desperately for a "magic cure." In a last-ditch effort to save a once-cherished relationship, they came to me for counseling. How can two people who once adored each other and wanted to grow old together end up at the crossroads of divorce? How indeed? And how will they handle the reality of divorce? Will they respond proactively or reactively? Will they see it as a learning opportunity through which they can grow, or will they retreat in bitterness and set themselves up for more disappointment and frustration and even toxic emotion and stress-related illness?

When it comes to marital problems, there are three possible outcomes. The first is to break up and learn nothing from the experience, in which case the parties set themselves up for repeat relationship failure. The other two possibilities are either to stay and learn, or leave and learn. The decision to stay in a difficult relationship or to leave one both offer learning opportunities that may be difficult, overwhelming and confusing. In the end, if the parties are proactive, they may also be empowering and edifying.

Divorce does not have to be destructive to either party. Of course it is easiest when the couple can come to an amicable agreement to bring a healthy resolution to the change in their relationship, especially when children are involved. When they are, the most important thing is for them to be protected. Ensuring the children's welfare should come before all other concerns. Unfortunately, many divorcing couples are too caught up in their own emotional distress to think clearly where their children are concerned.

It is important to protect the children because children of divorce commonly blame themselves for their parents' problems. Divorcing parents need to make sure that their children understand that the divorce is not their fault, nor is it of either parent. Divorce is a choice the parents make – a choice consistent with the law of nature that everything in fact is constantly changing. Sometimes, of course, two people can weather the changes together. Sometimes not. Either way, children must never be left feeling they are to blame.

# A Relationship Is Either Growing or Dying

I commonly tell couples that relationships are either dying or growing. There is no in-between and nothing remains healthy long in a state of stagnation. When one person in a relationship continues to grow personally, relationally or even occupationally while the other does not, their relationship is destined to hit a wall at some point, a point I call the crisis point.

Mutual accountability should be an understood part of any healthy marriage relationship because a husband and wife depend on each other in countless ways. Understanding and accepting the ebb and flow of life can secure for a couple the journey of relational longevity. It's important to balance the good days, weeks, months and years with those that are not so good, remembering that no relationship and no person is perfect. In this life of beginnings and endings we can't afford to take anything for granted, especially marriage. Open, honest and clear communication is an absolute must to keep a marriage vibrant and healthy over the long term. The secret longings of the heart must be shared often and clearly to keep the bonds of intimacy strong.

Living younger longer in relationships begins with knowing how to live younger longer in the midst of the stress. This knowledge enables us to live with the simplicity, power and passion to experience life to its fullest.

TERRY LYLES, PH.D.

# ✦ *Good Stress In Action...*

Evaluate your own personal grief recovery process. What are you grieving? What stage of grief are you in? Is there anything else you can do to help yourself manage the process of grief? Remember, the ability to handle stress is lower during times of grief. At times like this, life may seem overwhelming, which is why it is especially important to get help from friends, family and qualified professionals.

# Epilogue

The journey home from any disaster relief effort can be profoundly stressful and even confusing. You look forward to home and family and normalcy, but your heart, mind and body are still resonating with the horrors you've just witnessed – the lives lost, relationships severed, homes, property and natural areas destroyed. Even as the airplane lifted into the clouds over Bangkok and I knew that within hours family and friends would greet me with a warm welcome, my emotions raced from guilt to sorrow to relief and back to guilt again.

The last leg of the flight from Los Angeles to South Florida was particularly painful as I tried to grasp all that had happened and to write down my thoughts, feelings and impressions. Images flooded my mind: the wall covered with thousands of photos of missing babies and adults...the many destroyed villages...the mud-caked survivors in tattered clothes, children without parents...huge boats swept two miles inland...the sea floating with odd things like suitcases and Starbucks coffee machines...full-grown palm trees washed out to sea.

And would I ever forget the smells? Decaying corpses of the temple morgue mixed with Thai cooking at the "coffin café"...fetid water...rotting food and stinking soil.

This volatile mix of images, smells and emotions exploded in me even as I gazed at the peaceful sky outside the aircraft window. Although I knew that I could never erase them from my heart, I also knew that my tsunami relief experiences would give me a greater ability to inspire other disaster survivors with hope and the assurance of better days ahead.

My long flights to and from Thailand were shared with Hollywood action star Jean-Claude Van Damme, who came to Bangkok to help raise support for tsunami victims. Jean-Claude was a bright spot in my three-week Thailand trip. He reminded me of less stressful moments watching him in his wild and wonderful action films. Of course it's easier to watch destruction in a movie than to actually witness its effects, as I did in Phuket. But the philosophy of good stress teaches that every stressful situation can be positive and beneficial in the long run. Every stressful situation has moments of learning and growth, what I call teachable moments. I had many of these in Thailand and I expect to have many more along life's journey.

There isn't a day that passes that I don't think about Wat Yan Yao with its extremely hot and steamy conditions, its death and devastation a pungent reality all around me. Every day I count my blessings knowing that each day is a gift to be enjoyed to the fullest.

Living younger longer is about enjoying the moments of each day. It's about understanding the awesome privilege we have to learn from our experiences and to share them with other people. Growing older is a true gift when you think of all the people who die young. Living each day with your end in view can crystallize your daily goals and keep them in focus. Start each day with purpose and reflect on your unique reason for being on the planet. Stay connected to this vitally important process. It can provide the most powerful trigger release of passion and motivation to conquer each day.

Many people lose their motivation to explore and accomplish in life because they are disconnected from their life purpose and destiny. If we can simply let life develop around us, we can be inspired to pursue our dreams and aspirations. Inspiration is within all of us from birth, and manifests through spiritual connectedness to God, self, and others. Acting upon this can transform our lives.

When thoughts and beliefs align, powerful things happen. The first is an overwhelming sense of peace and fulfillment. The second is the conviction that our thoughts and beliefs shape our actions, and that these actions lead to a new reality.

When I finally arrived back at my office and sat down in the same seat in which I had been sitting only a few weeks before, I realized how much I had changed. It was the same office that my colleague Chris Galli had called only three weeks before to tell me about the tsunami, but now it looked and felt so different. During my time in Thailand, Chris had called regularly, knowing that I often felt alone and cut off from the rest of the world. Now I called him and related my mixed feelings to him – quite a bit different than the driven excitement a few weeks earlier, before my departure for Thailand.

I realized that I had come full circle from that day, and the difference was that my circle had grown enormously. Those few weeks in Thailand had given me what felt like years of learning. It was truly a life-changing experience, and taught me to be aware of the gift of today, and to never take anything for granted.

Life is precious and fleeting. Enjoying each day to the fullest by aligning with our life purpose can make living younger longer a golden reality. Living gracefully also means living with no regrets and without looking back in remorse. The past is gone and the future beckons seductively, waiting for us to write our destiny across its pristine pages.

Balance is beautiful. Think of a ballerina poised on the tip of a toe, body thrust forward, arms spread like an eagle's wings. Balance is the key to life; balance is what this book is all about. By balancing stress with recovery, we can experience stress as a positive force that enables us to live younger longer. By balancing the mental, emotional, spiritual, and physical dimensions of life, we can live life to its utmost. Balance should not be something we strive for, but a way of living every day of our lives for optimum health and elite performance. Balance is not a destination but a journey, the journey of life. Although the road may be bumpy and sometimes dark, there's always a spectacular sunrise on the horizon.

TERRY LYLES CORPORATION

TERRY LYLES, PH.D.

AMERICA'S
STRESS
DOCTOR

*Dear Reader:*

Congratulations on having completed *Good Stress* and learning useful skills and tools for using stress to accomplish positive outcomes in your life. As you now know, the secret to *Good Stress* is found in the alignment of *mental, emotional, spiritual* and *physical* capacities, combined with proper work/rest cycles at home and at work. The backdrop of this unique technology stems from sports science and performance psychology that has worked for thousands of individuals in every area of life. Within these next few pages are the various forms of training through consulting, workshops, audio and video resources that could be just what the doctor ordered for maintaining high levels of performance in your life. These products and services will help you navigate life and all its storms. Welcome to the next step; I look forward to serving you and salute your continued success.

**Terry Lyles**

"I have been through many storms in my life and thought that I had learned the answers about dealing with them... I realized how much more I needed to learn after working with Terry's program. I know that you'll feel the same way after reading this powerful material."

**Pat Williams**
*Senior Vice President*
Orlando Magic

## Order Your FREE
## Stress Recovery Manual Today
## by visiting www.terrylyles.com

The Stress Recovery Manual was a blessing in the wake of a record-setting 2005 hurricane season. Dr. Terry Lyles, America's Stress Doctor, donated thousands of hours to the volunteers, victims and heroes of **Hurricanes Katrina, Rita** and **Wilma** – people who were subjected to enormous amounts of hardship and challenge.

Now you can benefit from his time-tested and scientifically-measured approach to stress utilization.

"This manual is applicable to anyone wanting to improve their relationship to stress," says Dr. Lyles, who for the past 10 years has trained hundreds of individuals, including fire rescue workers in and around **Ground Zero**, international forensic medical teams in **tsunami-torn Asia**, and those affected by this year's **hurricanes**. Dr. Lyles has also trained top executives, managers and employees in Fortune 500 companies and the U.S. Government as well as professional athletes.

# Services

## Sports Training

Human performance measurement in the field of sport science is unique and well-documented. Understanding the limits of the human body and how to maximize and conserve energy levels before, during, and after performance is the key to consistent results. The mind/body alignment process is the secret to entering the ZONE under pressure, on demand with consistent results.

Routines before, during and after performance must be coupled with oscillatory stress/recovery cycles that align specifically to each performance or event. Using a performance coach can shorten the learning curve for healthy change and secure the desired results that elite performers worldwide expect and deserve. This program is for adults and youth.

## Family Training

Family is a high priority for Dr. Lyles, who has two teenage boys, the eldest an eighteen-year-old quadriplegic. Whether married, separated or divorced, mutual respect, dignity and empowering communication are the keys for lifelong family relationships. The *Navigating Family Chaos* program is a humorous and enlightening program filled with cutting-edge technology and practical everyday life experiences. Young people today are faced with violence and threats within neighborhoods and schools nationwide. Marriages and blended families are challenged as never before, causing confusion and frustration with few answers. Learn how a family that works together to maintain daily balance and alignment can overcome tremendous odds and experience relational and family success.

## Corporate Training

The Terry Lyles Corporation (TLC) specializes in corporate human-performance enhancement. We have researched and refined training protocols in the areas of stress utilization, fitness, nutrition and physiology. Our cutting edge, state-of-the-art corporate leadership training program, *Navigating Life Storms,* challenges, educates and motivates both employers and employees toward successful implementation of the corporate vision.

Vision is often blurred by deadlines, budgets, quotas, production and competition. These factors are affected by goals, expectations, demands, inability to meet production and diminished product quality. Vision is then tabled in favor of responding to immediate crises, which results in a sacrifice of quality. We've learned that if you don't have time to do it right the first time, you will have to make time to do it over. With our program, employees act as teams to develop the necessary skills to turn pressure into opportunity and thereby get excellent results in less than optimal circumstances – *under pressure and on demand.*

TLC offers multi-dimensional educational and training curriculum involving individuals at every level of the organization. Our technology has been implemented in professional and amateur athletics, Fortune 100 and 500 companies, law enforcement, aviation training, fire-rescue workers and military special-forces training. Executives and management teams alike rely upon its solid, scientifically measurable, time-tested and proven training, which yields improved communication skills, productivity, retention and loyalty through stress utilization.

## LIFE COACHING

Sport Coaching has been around for a long time, producing measurable performance results in less time primarily because if you are *in* the game, you cannot *see* the game! Coaches do not produce talent and skill; instead, they help improve an individual's talent and skill to take performance to a higher level.

The use of coaches and instructors for music, physical conditioning and martial arts is nothing new, but have you ever considered a life coach to help you achieve personal, relational and occupational success? If not, consider Your Coach For Life – America's Stress Doctor – Dr. Terry Lyles, who coaches executives, athletes, and aspiring performers to unearth talent and skill to redefine life pursuits and increase health, happiness and productivity.

# TRAINING MANUALS FROM TERRY LYLES CORPORATION

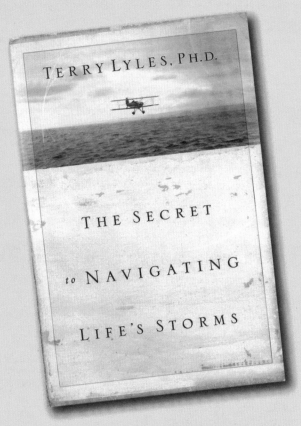

## THE SECRET TO NAVIGATING LIFE'S STORMS – AUTOGRAPHED BOOK

This book assists parents, families, executives and elite performers in the quest for living life to the fullest each day, without losing personal health, happiness and daily productivity. *The Secret to Navigating Life's Storms* is a collection of inspiring and uplifting stories from years of work with professional athletes, corporate executives, military Special Forces, and the professionals and volunteers at Ground Zero. Dr. Lyles also shares his own personal stories of raising two children, one who is quadriplegic and wheelchair bound for twenty years, and shares how he empowered and motivated himself and those around him to remain optimistic about what is truly possible through the correct utilization of daily stress. Dr. Lyles' honest and humorous approach is both touching and engaging, providing us an excellent framework for handling stress well in any situation. $12.53

# NAVIGATING LIFE'S STORMS TRAINING KIT

Get the complete Navigating Life Storms CD/DVD series today.
• 2 DVD's
• 5 Audio CD's
• An Interactive CD Rom

**Navigating Life Storms DVDs**
This two-part DVD series is packed with ninety minutes of fast-moving but pointed information related to stress utilization as it relates to: why diets don't work, why exercise isn't fun, why emotions are commonly misunderstood, why daily confusion is so common and why sleep is often interrupted by the last meal of the day. This powerful training experience is suitable for adults as well as adolescents who are interested in learning how to use daily stress as a stimulus for growth instead of allowing its negative force to interfere with our success.

**Five Part Audio Collection**
This five-part audio CD collection is designed to support the CD ROM, DVD and written material while driving in the car, working out or walking around the house, for deeper understanding and integration. These CDs are for the participant who wishes to fully transform their experience of converting stress into a powerful stimulus for growth and healthy change, taking their lifestyle to a whole new level.

For more information on these and other TLC products, visit
www.terrylyles.com

## VIRTUAL STRESS DOCTOR INTERACTIVE CD ROM

This Interactive program is designed to interface with a computer for an up-close and interactive experience with Dr. Lyles. This interactive features five intro video clips, covering each section of the book "The Secret of Navigating Life's Storms," and five separate audio clips that interface with a preloaded PowerPoint presentation that coaches the participant to a more in-depth learning experience on handling mental, emotional, spiritual, and physical stress daily. This unique training technology can be stopped and started with the PowerPoint program and also printed off and recorded just like the corporate executives who receive private coaching from Dr. Lyles.

# TERRY LYLES
## FOUNDATION

The Terry Lyles Foundation was established to help individuals and families recover from life disasters and misfortunes as a result of an unforeseen natural event such as a hurricane, a Tsuanmi, an earthquake, or a national tragedy such as 9/11. Your tax-deductible donations fund critical support to help victims of disasters rebuild and reestablish their lives in times of devastation. Please contact us through our website www.TerryLyles.com to make a contribution. Your support has never been more important.

Coretta Scott King
and Dr. Terry Lyles

"Stress is good for us. Our bodies are hard-wired to handle stress. Properly utilized, stess can propel us toward success in every area of life. Stress is meant to define us, not defeat us; to illuminate us, not eliminate us; to complement our lives, not complicate them."

– Dr. Terry Lyles